Academic Presenting and Presentations

Student's Book

Further components in this series

Teachers' Book: ISBN 978-1-911369-25-7

Downloadable videos: www.linguabooks.com/app

www.linguabooks.com

Academic Presenting and Presentations

A preparation course for university students

Student's Book

PETER LEVRAI

AVERIL BOLSTER

Academic Presenting and Presentations
A preparation course for university students

Student's Book

Peter Levrai and Averil Bolster have asserted
their right under the Copyright, Designs and
Patents Act, 1988 to be identified as the authors of this work.

ISBN: 978-1-911369-24-0

Second edition

Editor: Ann Claypole

Proofreader: Marie-Christin Strobel

Copyright © 2015, 2019 LinguaBooks

Every effort has been made to trace the holders of intellectual property rights and the publishers will be happy to correct any mistakes or omissions in future editions.

Special thanks are due to the following for permission to reproduce scholarly articles: R. Taflinger ('Introduction To Research'), C. R. Kothari ('Research Methodology - An Introduction'), B. Quarton ('Research Skills And The New Undergraduate') and the British Library ('Tips for Researching').

'Research Skills and the New Undergraduate' was previously published in the *Journal of Instructional Psychology* Vol. 30, No. 2, June 2003.

'Research Methodology - An Introduction' was previously published in *Research Methodology: Methods & Techniques* by C. R. Kothari, New Age International (P) Ltd., New Delhi, 2004.

All rights reserved. No part of this publication may be reproduced, stored in a retrieval system or transmitted, in any form or by any means, electronic, mechanical, photocopying, recording or otherwise, without the prior permission of the publishers.

A CIP catalogue record for this book is available from the British Library.

This book is sold subject to the condition that it shall not, by way of trade or otherwise, be lent, re-sold, hired out or otherwise circulated without the publisher's prior consent in any form of binding or cover other than that in which it is published and without a similar condition including this condition being imposed on the subsequent purchaser.

LinguaBooks
Elsie Whiteley Innovation Centre
Hopwood Lane
Halifax HX1 5ER

www.linguabooks.com

Contents

Foreword 9

Introduction 11
   Who this course is for 11
   How to use this course 11
   Learning Presentations and Sample Presentations 11
   Scope and content 12

Course Overview 13

Learning Presentations 14

Sample Presentations 15

Unit 1 Introduction to Presentations 17
   Welcome to Academic Presenting and Presentations 18
   Presentation tip 19
   A good presentation 21
   Staying focused 21
   Having A POINT 22

Unit 2 What is an Academic Presentation? 25
   Presenting at university 26
   Identifying an academic presentation 27
   Features of an academic presentation 28
   Organising language 1 31
   Use of stress 31
   Repetition of words 31
   Organising language 2 32
   Summarising a presentation 33
   Explaining ideas 33
   Describing data 1 33
   Organising language 3 34
   Describing data 2 35

Unit 3 Presenting a Paper 37
Academic focus – research 38
Presenting a paper 45

Project Introduction – Approaching A Topic 53
Organising language 4 55
Talking about a paper 55
Reacting to a paper 56

Unit 4 Elevator Pitch Poster Presentations 57
Working in groups 58
Poster presentations 61
Elevator pitch presentations 63
Overcoming nerves 64
Outlining structure 67
Rhetorical questions 67
Introducing background 67
Directing the audience's attention 67
Explaining difficult terminology 67
Emphasising points 67

Unit 5 Persuasive Presentations 69
Research methods 72
Opening with a question 75
Referring to sources 75
Presenting your position 75
Providing examples 75
Discussing advantages 76
Discussing disadvantages 76

Unit 6 Presenting Progress 79

Project Review – Giving A Progress Presentation 85
Explaining how your project started 86
Describing research 86
Explaining methodology 86
Describing outcomes 86

Unit 7 Problem/Solution Presentations 89
- Citing and referencing 93
- Presentation planning 94
- Defining terms 96
- Explaining importance 96
- Moving between sections 96
- Discussing solutions 96

Unit 8 Research Presentations 99

Project Presentation – Giving A Final Presentation 106
- Explaining a research topic 107
- Explaining methodology 107
- Explaining findings 108
- Discussing limitations 108
- Discussing conclusions and implications 108
- Introducing future research topics 108

Worksheets 111

How to use the worksheets 112
- Preparation 113
- General Feedback 114
- Overall Assessment 115
- Non-verbal Communication 116
- Visual Aids 117
- Body Language and Delivery 118
- Dealing with Questions 119
- Academic Integrity 120
- Planning 121
- Audience Profile 122
- Notecard Template 123

*Simplicity is the
greatest sophistication*

Leonardo Da Vinci

Foreword

Oral Presentations are an important part of studying in an English-medium university environment and will be something many students face, whatever their field of study. Such presentations can be particularly challenging for non-native English speakers and consequently they need support to develop their academic presentation skills.

Academic Presenting and Presentations (APP) is a research-based training course designed to help students cultivate academic presentation skills and deal with the various presentation tasks they may have to do as part of their university studies. The material is suitable for a global audience and can be used in a wide range of contexts in the field of EAP (English for Academic Purposes), since it helps develop presentation skills and also deals with broader topics of interest in a study-oriented context such as research and plagiarism. The material emphasises higher level task-achievement rather than discrete language points since experience shows that this is the area that most students find especially difficult.

A key tenet of the course is that effective presentation skills alone will not lead to a successful academic presentation. More than technical presentation skills, students will also have to appreciate the key features of academic presentations (such as soundness of argument or use of referenced support) and also be aware of the expectations of different genres of academic presentation, from seminar presentations introducing a paper to more sophisticated research presentations. Each unit of Academic Presenting and Presentations therefore focuses on a different presentation genre, building students' awareness of not only how to present effectively, but of how to present appropriately in an academic environment.

Also, as it is a presentation course, the accompanying videos form an integral component of this course. The videos consist of two types of presentation: *Learning Presentations,* which give advice to students and *Sample Presentations,* which illustrate different types of presentation.

The presentations are available online and can be found on the Academic Presenting and Presentations website at:

http://www.linguabooks.com/app

Further notes, guidance for class work and details of the theoretical rationale are provided in the accompanying Teacher's Book.

The authors and publishers would like to thank Naeema Hann, Heather Buchanan, Martyn Bingham, Lisa Warner, Brian Tomlinson, Patrick Hafenstein, Ron White and faculty and colleagues at the University of Nottingham Ningbo China and also Marie-Christin Strobel for valuable assistance at the proofreading stage.

Introduction

Welcome to **Academic Presenting and Presentations**, a course to help university students develop their presentation skills in a range of different types of presentation.

Who this course is for

This course is for any student who has to give a presentation as part of their studies, either in the shape of informal seminar presentation tasks or more formal assessed presentations. It is also designed to be used by either native or non-native English speakers, with an English-language focus to help those presenting through a foreign language.

How to use this course

Each unit of the course focuses on a different type of presentation task so that the material can be used in any order but it is best used linearly as skills are built up and developed over several units. The accompanying videos can be found at http://www.linguabooks.com/app.

If you wish to view the presentations using a standard DVD player instead of a computer, a set of Video DVDs can be ordered from the publishers.

Learning Presentations and Sample Presentations

APP contains both *Learning Presentations* and *Sample Presentations*. The Learning Presentations speak directly to you, giving advice and suggestions about presenting. The Sample Presentations give you the opportunity to see different types of presentation in practice and identify successful elements you can use to develop your own presentations. There is an analysis of each Sample

Presentation at the end of each unit, looking at the organisation, language and an overall evaluation of the presentation.

Scope and content

Each unit contains an average of two hours of input material (presentations to watch, class discussions, language exercises, etc.). It is expected that this will take approximately one third of the course time. The rest of the time will be spent on presentation preparation, presentation practice and feedback.

The best way to learn about presenting is to present as much and as often as possible and also to watch different people present to see what works and what does not.

Course Overview

Unit	Topic	Presentation skill	Language skill	Academic skill
1 Introduction to Presentations	Presentation Skills	Basic presentation structure	Signposting Language	
2 What is an Academic Presentation?	Academic Presentations	Identifying good presentation techniques	Noticing useful language Pronunciation Skills – developing a presentation voice	Recognising what makes a presentation academic
3 Seminar Presentations 1: Presenting a Paper	What is Research?	Referring to the work of others	Using the language of stance	Summarising a short paper Synthesising papers
	Project Introduction	Approaching A Topic		
4 Elevator Pitch Poster Presentations	Teamwork	Developing clear visual aids	Diplomatic language	Teamwork and group presentations
5 Persuasive Presentations	Research Methodologies	Changing the mind of the audience	Persuasive language	Evaluating your argument
6 Seminar Presentations 2: Presenting Progress	Smartphone Project Presentation	Using presentation software	Talking about the past and future	Giving a project progress report Dealing with questions
	Project Review	Giving A Progress Presentation		
7 Problem/ Solution Presentations	Plagiarism	Presenting without a script	Paraphrasing	Avoiding plagiarism Referencing
8 Presenting Research	Research Presentations	Presenting data	Describing tables and graphs	Finding sources
	Project Presentation	Giving A Final Presentation		

Learning Presentations

These presentations are designed to give you useful information and advice about the different presentation tasks you might be asked to carry out as part of your studies.

Unit	Presentation Title
1	1.1 – **Introduction To Presentations** – The Basics
	1.2 – **What Makes A Good Presentation** – Making Sure Your Presentation Has A POINT
	1.3 – **Presentation Task** – Presentations and Me
2	2.1 – **The Academic Presentation** – Key Features of Academic Presentations
	2.2 – **Presentation As Performance** – Developing Your Presentation Voice
3	3.1 – **Presenting A Paper** – Make Your Opinion Known
	3.2 – **Presenting More Than One Paper** – Horizontal vs. Vertical
4	4.1 – **Group Presentations** – Everyone Has A Role
	4.2 – **Designing A Poster** – Making An Impact
	4.3 – **Elevator Pitch Presentations** – Making A Point in 30 Seconds or Less
5	5.1 – **Being Persuasive In An Academic Presentation** – Substance Over Style
6	6.1 – **Presenting Progress** – Two Approaches
	6.2 – **Using Presentation Software** – Helping the Audience Follow Your Message
7	7.1 – **Problem/Solution Presentations** – Cause and Effect
8	8.1 – **Presenting Data** – Statistics, Tables and Graphs
	8.2 – **Research Presentations** – Finding and Filling A Gap

Sample Presentations

These presentations give you an opportunity to see different types of presentation in order to identify what works and what doesn't. A review of each Sample Presentation can be found at the end of each unit.

Unit	Presentation Title
2	**2A – Electric Vehicles –** The way to a brighter future?
	2B – An Evaluation of Barriers to Electric Car Use
	2C – The Ion Plus – Finus Sales Report and Projections
3	**3A – Introduction to Research –** 3 Types of Research
	3B – Research Methodology: An Introduction – The Objectives And Motivations of Research
	3C – What is Research?
4	**4A – Managing Teamwork –** Roles and Responsibilities
5	**5A – Electric Vehicles –** The way to a brighter future (*Presentation 2A*)
	5B – Choosing a Research Method – Striking A Balance
6	**6A – Are Smartphones Destroying Language?**
7	**7A – Avoiding Plagiarism –** Citing and Note-making
8	**8A – Undergraduate Research Methods –** Using Online and Library Sources

In order to make this course easier to use, **Learning Presentations** are introduced like this:

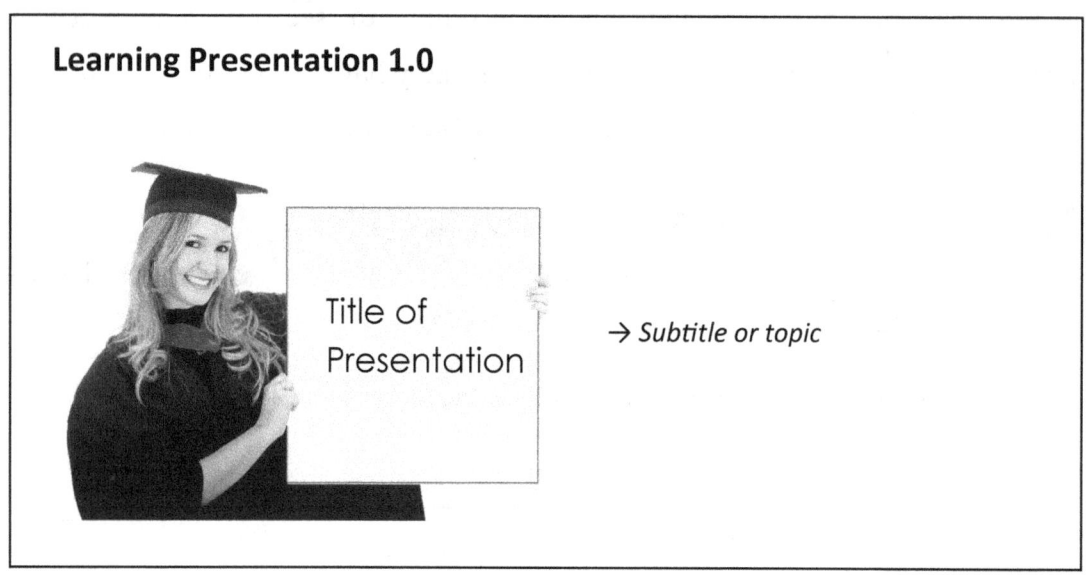

And **Sample Presentations** are identified like this:

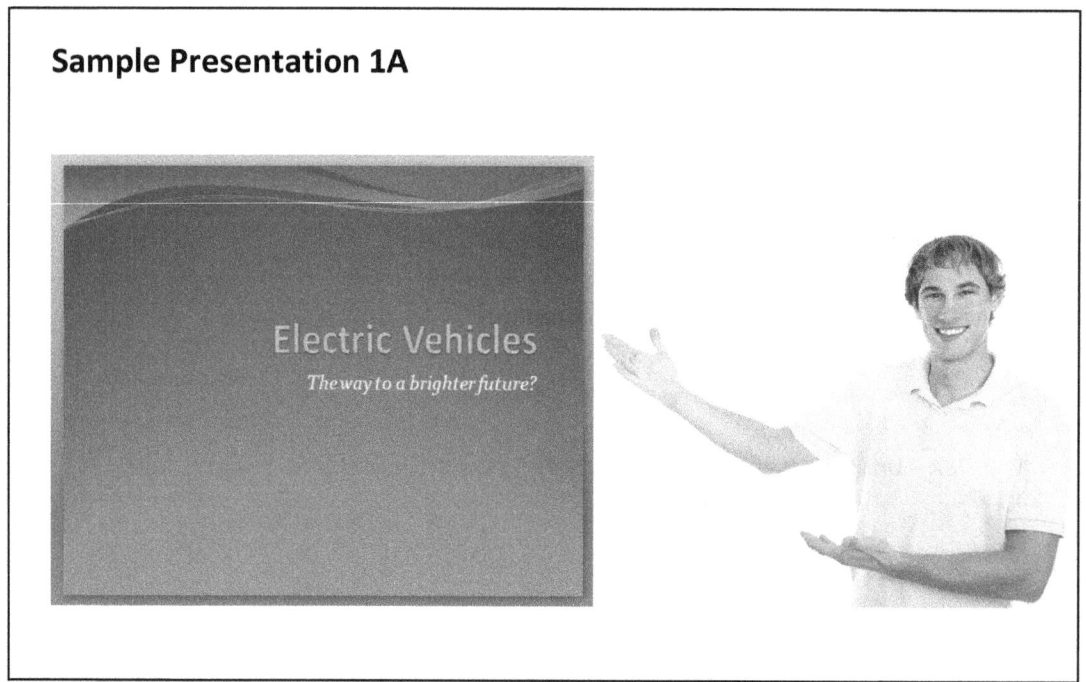

Unit 1
Introduction to Presentations

Unit 1 Introduction to Presentations

Unit Aims
Each unit of this course is designed to help you answer some questions about presentations. Take a look at the questions below and discuss the answers.

- When do people give presentations?
- Why do people give presentations?
- What makes a good presentation?

At the end of the unit, return to these questions and see how much your answers may have changed or developed.

Welcome to Academic Presenting and Presentations

Presenting is a very useful skill at university and beyond. However, a lot of people dislike presenting or are even afraid of presenting. But anyone can learn how to present well and *Academic Presenting and Presentations* is designed to help you understand what is expected in the various types of presentation you may be asked to give as part of your studies, from informal seminar presentations to formal assessed end-of-term presentations.

Before getting started there is a very important piece of advice. During the course you will have many opportunities to present in front of your classmates. **Take every chance you can**. Developing your presentation skills only comes through doing presentations and the only way to become comfortable presenting is to do it as much as possible. The secrets to being a good presenter are:

Learning Presentation 1.1

→ *The Basics*

Throughout this course you will come across different **Learning Presentations** which will give you tips and advice about giving presentations. These short presentations are designed to give you the information you need to help you prepare and deliver better academic presentations. They will also model some useful structures and language that you can use in your own presentations. The first **Learning Presentation** provides an overview of the course. As you watch, make notes of any interesting points.

Presentation tip

In the presentation you were advised to pay attention to the presentations you watch in order to pick up useful ideas about organisation, language and delivery. For example, in the presentation you have just seen you could think about the structure. In the presentation the speaker:

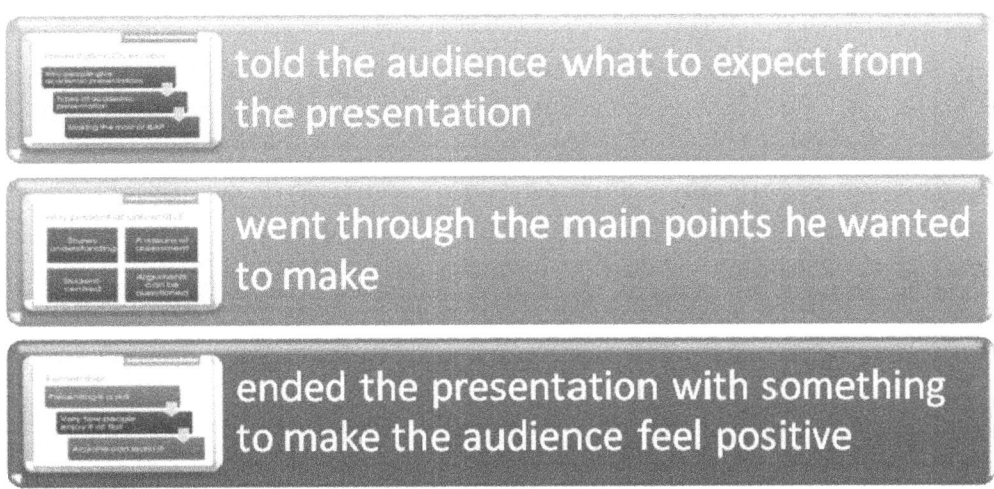

Language Focus

Signposting Language
The presentation also talked about signposting language, i.e. language you can use to make sure the audience can follow your presentation.

Throughout this course you will see a lot of different presentations and will hear a lot of different signposting language. It's a good idea to have a presentation notebook where you can record any useful phrases into categories, as illustrated below.

Stating Your Topic
I'd like to talk about...
I'm going to begin by...
I'm going to tell you about...

Sequencing
First ...
After that ...
Finally ...

Moving between sections
Now ...
Having looked at (x), we can now move on to consider (y).
Turning to ...

Signposting language also helps you as a presenter to keep track of where you are and what is coming next. The *Presentation Review* section at the back of this book highlights some of the useful language used in the **Sample Presentations**.

"I'm going to begin by giving you a brief outline of my topic."

A good presentation

A presentation is a combination of many different factors and to give an effective presentation all of those factors need to work together. A presentation is more than what someone says. It is also how they say it, how they look and how they move. It is how all of these things combine to make an enjoyable presentation. Note below what you think makes a good presentation.

A Good Presentation

Staying focused

It is important to remember that as a presenter you have a responsibility to the audience. You are taking their time so you should make good use of it and make sure your presentation is useful to them in some way. It could tell them something they didn't know before or make them think about something they are familiar with in a new light.

Learning Presentation 1.2

→ *Making Sure Your Presentation Has A POINT*

This Learning Presentation introduces a way to think about what makes a good presentation. As you watch add anything you agree with to your notes.

Having A POINT

The speaker talked about ensuring your presentation has A POINT.

Audience	Who is the presentation for? What do they need to know? What do they know already?
Purpose	What does the presenter want to achieve with the presentation?
Organisation	How is the presentation organised?
Impact	How does the presenter try to make an impact on the audience?
Notable	What are the key points of the presentation?
Theatre	How is the presentation delivered?

Presentation Task 1

You are now going to give a short presentation. The title of the task is *Presentations and Me* and you have to present who you are and say something about presentations.

Learning Presentation 1.3

→ *Presentations and Me*

Watch this Learning Presentation to get some ideas how to approach a task.

Remember, don't make the presentation too long and make sure listening to you is worth the audience's time.

Write an outline for the presentation you are going to give and also make a note of any useful phrases you want to remember to use.

Unit 2
What is an Academic Presentation?

Unit 2   What is an Academic Presentation?

Unit Aims
Each unit of this course is designed to help you answer some questions about academic presentations. Take a look at the questions below and discuss the answers.

- What different kinds of presentations do people have to do at university?
- What makes a presentation academic?
- How should you use your voice during a presentation?

At the end of the unit, return to these questions and see how much your answers may have changed or developed.

Presenting at university

There are a lot of different types of presentation you might be asked to do at university and there is no one way to approach any of them. An effective presenter is flexible. In this course there will be suggestions of how you might organise your presentations but the structure you choose will depend on what you are trying to achieve in your presentation and who the audience is. Before looking at different types of academic presentation, it is important to consider what makes a presentation academic. Make a note of your ideas below.

The Academic Presentation

Identifying an academic presentation

Sample Presentations 2A, 2B, 2C
As You Watch

You are going to watch three presentations. One of them is academic. As you watch decide which of the presentations is academic, and how you know. What makes a presentation academic? Add your ideas to your notes.

Sample Presentation 2A

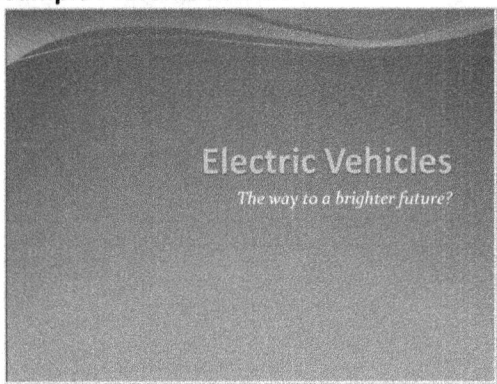

Sample Presentation 2B

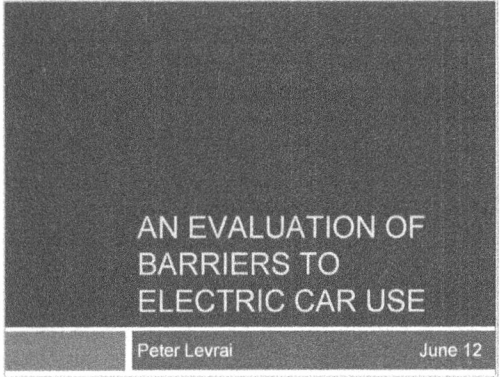

Sample Presentation 2C

> **Language Focus**
>
> It's important to start a presentation positively, as your energy and enthusiasm for your topic will affect your audience. If you do not seem interested, there is no reason for them to be. When you say 'Good morning' or 'Good afternoon' make sure you believe it. Make sure they believe it. Your presentation will be the best morning of their lives.
>
> Think about how the speakers introduced themselves and their topics. Make a note of any useful phrases in your presentation notebook. Include your thoughts about *how* they said what they said.

Learning Presentation 2.1

→ *Key Features of Academic Presentations*

Watch the next Learning Presentation and complete your notes about what makes a presentation academic.

Features of an academic presentation

In some general ways an academic presentation is the same as any other presentation. There is a presenter and an audience and the presenter is trying to affect the audience. There are, however, some things that make an academic presentation different to other types of presentation.

Academic presentations

- **usually answer a question**

    In the Sample Presentation you watched, the question was to evaluate the barriers to the spread of electric cars.

- **are supported by references**

    As in an essay, it is very important to show how your ideas fit into, and build on, the ideas of experts you have come across in your reading.

- **develop an argument**

    This does not mean argument in the sense of disagreeing and fighting with someone. Academic argument is the logical exploration of an idea.

Learning Presentation 2.2

→ *Developing Your Presentation Voice*

The way you present is very important. Think about the way the speaker in Sample Presentation 2A used their voice to emphasise points and try to influence the audience. Discuss what you should do about these things:

- Speed
- Hesitation
- Stress
- Intonation

Watch the next Learning Presentation for tips about considering presenting as performing.

Language Focus

You need to remember that your voice is a powerful presenting tool. You are not talking, you are presenting and you should use a presentation voice. Generally in a presentation, because the audience is bigger than in a normal conversation, your voice needs to be more powerful.

Look at the short presentation below and practice saying it. Before you do, think *how* you are going to say it to make an impression on the audience. Where are the stresses going to be? Where will you pause? You can mark the text to remind you what you want to do with your voice. Try out various combinations and see what difference they make.

Good morning ladies and gentlemen. Thank you for giving me some of your time today. My name is ... and I am here today to talk to you about giving presentations. Presenting is a valuable skill to develop and today I'm going to tell you the secret of giving a good presentation.

Of course, many things contribute to giving a good presentation. There is the preparation you do, how much you know about the topic and what you have to say about it. It's also important to make sure your visual aids help you in the presentation and help the audience follow what you are saying.

Giving a good presentation means that you have a clear message and, more importantly, understand how to get that message across to the people in your audience in a way they will understand. But more than all of these, more than your preparation, more than your use of visuals, more than your knowledge of the audience and the message you want to give them, I believe that the single most important thing in giving a good presentation is confidence. It's having the confidence to stand up in front of a room of strangers and believing you have something interesting and important to tell them. It's the confidence to deliver your presentation with conviction, to sound as if you know what you are talking about and there is a good reason for people to listen to you.

Confidence, ladies and gentlemen, that's the secret to presenting.

Review of SP 2A – Electric Vehicles

This is a persuasive presentation, delivered to a general public audience with the intention of making them think electric cars are not a good idea.

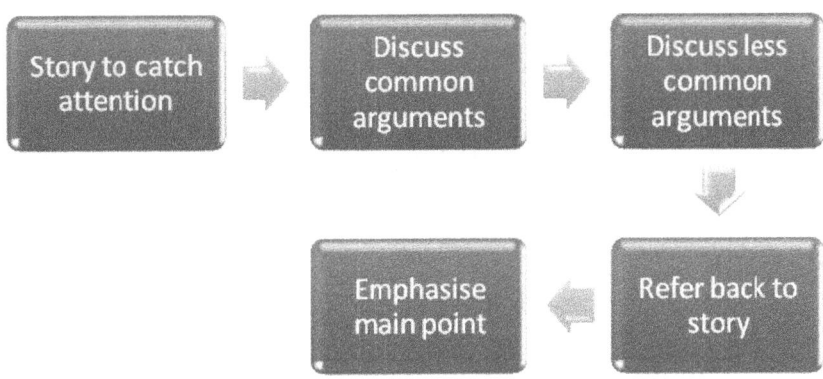

Organising language 1

Today I'm here to talk about … and whether …

Before I begin my presentation today, I'd like to …

So today I want to be talking about …

(There are) a few reasons that you'll probably be aware of that I want to talk about in a little bit more detail.

But I think the main reason …

To close my presentation today, I'd like to …

Use of stress

*Sue has done **a lot** of work*

*They had **everything** planned and started the journey to the hospital. **But** …*

Repetition of words

Batteries are a dirty business … dirty to extract, dirty to process and dirty to dispose of.

Comment

This is a presentation that tries to work on the audience's emotion by using the story of Bob and Sue. Their story is not just used in the introduction, but referred back to in the body of the presentation and in the conclusion. While it is effective, it lacks any kind of support and needs more evidence, particularly around the arguments to do with the pollution caused by batteries. Why should we believe the presenter? Where's the evidence?

Review of SP 2B – An Evaluation of Barriers to Electric Car Use

This is an academic presentation, perhaps given as part of an assignment. The speaker analyses the different reasons why electric cars are not more popular.

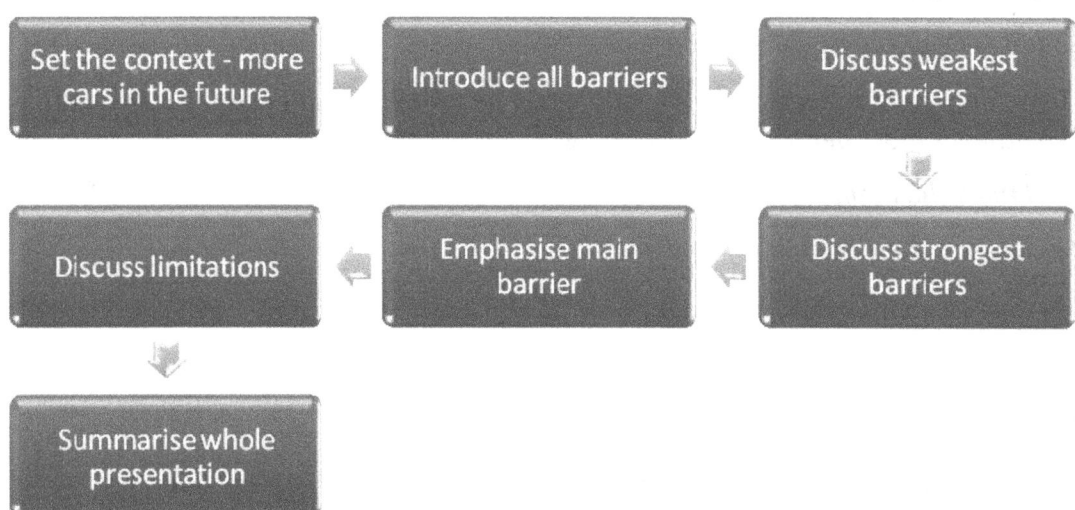

Organising language 2

Good afternoon ladies and gentlemen. My name's ... and today I'm here to talk to you about ...

My presentation's going to take about ten minutes and there'll be time at the end for questions so please leave any questions you may have until then.

I'm going to be talking first of all ...

I'll be moving on to consider ...

My presentation is going to close with ...

Before we get to that ...

Summarising a presentation

But to bring you to the end of my presentation ...

We talked about ...

I discussed ...

And I concluded that ...

Explaining ideas

I would also argue ...

I mentioned earlier ...

I say this because ...

And that's why I think ...

Describing data 1

This shows ...

This chart comes from data in a report by Lee and Lovett published in 2011 and as you can see ...

"And that's why I think we should act now before it is too late."

Review of SP 2C – The Ion Plus

This is an internal business presentation giving sales data about an electric car the company produces.

> **Comment**
>
> *This presentation starts out well supported but when discussing the four barriers, more support would be needed. The decision to divide the four barriers into strong and weak is a good one and the presentation logically goes from what the speaker sees as the weakest barrier, to the strongest.*

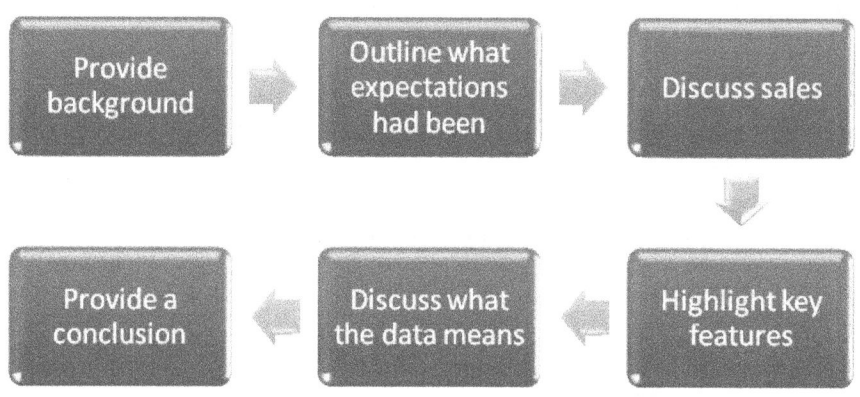

Organising language 3

Ok. Thank you for coming. Today I'm here to talk about … and …

Before getting into this in any detail, I'd like to remind you …

However, having said that …

Which brings me to my next slide …

More interestingly than that …

Describing data 2

This chart shows ...

There was a steady decline in ...

As you can see ...

This second chart ...

The projected Ion sales are shown in the light blue, the actual sales in the dark blue.

> **Comment**
>
> This is a data-based presentation in which graphs are used so the audience can follow the presentation easily. When talking about the graphs, the speaker doesn't go into a lot of detail but highlights main features and trends. Although the sales are worse than expected, the speaker is able to present them in a positive way.

"The positive aspect is that things are getting worse at a much slower rate than before."

Unit 3
Presenting a Paper

Unit 3 Seminar Presentations 1: *Presenting a Paper*

Unit Aims

As part of a seminar, you might be asked to present a paper or journal article you have read.

- What are you expected to say about a paper?
- How do you present two or more papers at the same time?
- What is stance and how can you show it in your language?

At the end of the unit, return to these questions and see how much your answers may have changed or developed.

Academic focus – research

In this unit you will be reading and watching presentations about research. It may seem early to start thinking about research but it is an important part of studying. Research can be as simple as using the library and internet to find more information about a subject. It can also involve doing some kind of investigation yourself to find out some information you can't find in books or journals. The important thing to remember about research is that you are doing it to answer a very specific question, and as you research it's important to have that question in mind all the time in order to stay focused on what you are trying to find out.

To find out more about research, read the two extracts below and make notes in the margin of any points you find of particular interest.

Text 1

Introduction To Research

By R Taflinger

from: http://public.wsu.edu/~taflinge/research.html

Information, ideas and opinions surround us, most of which we never question. In fact, we have to ignore most of them or suffer from brain burnout. However, when we do pay attention we usually accept it as it comes in from whatever source. For example, do you ever wonder if you're getting the whole story from TV news shows or newspapers? Do you wonder what's been left out, if anything? Or why? However, if we wish to understand something, not just accept someone else's word for it but actually understand it, and in turn pass on our understanding to someone else, we must question opinion and assumption and theory and speculation. The purpose of the questions is to gather evidence.

WHAT IS RESEARCH?
Research is finding out what you don't already know. No one knows everything, but everybody knows something. However, to complicate matters, often what you know, or think you know, is incorrect.

There are two basic purposes for research: to learn something, or to gather evidence. The first, to learn something, is for your own benefit. It is almost impossible for a human to stop learning. It may be the theory of relativity or the RBIs of your favorite ball player, but you continue to learn. Research is organized learning, looking for specific things to add to your store of knowledge. You may read SCIENTIFIC AMERICAN for the latest research in quantum mechanics, or the sports section for last night's game results. Either is research.

What you've learned is the source of the background information you use to communicate with others. In any conversation you talk about the things you know, the things you've learned. If you know nothing about the subject under discussion, you can neither contribute nor understand it. (This fact does not, however, stop many people from joining in on conversations, anyway.) When you write or speak formally, you share what you've learned with others, backed with evidence to show that what you've learned is correct. If, however, you haven't learned more than your audience already knows, there is nothing for you to share. Thus you do research.

NOTES

THREE TYPES OF RESEARCH

There are three types of research, pure, original, and secondary. Each type has the goal of finding information and/or understanding something. The difference comes in the strategy employed in achieving the objective.

Pure Research

Pure research is research done simply to find out something by examining anything. For instance, in some pure scientific research scientists discover what properties various materials possess. It is not for the sake of applying those properties to anything in particular, but simply to find out what properties there are. Pure mathematics is for the sake of seeing what happens, not to solve a problem.

The fun of pure research is that you are not looking for anything in particular. Instead, anything and everything you find may be joined with anything else just to see where that combination would lead, if anywhere.

Let's take an example. I was reading a variety of books and magazines once. There were some science fiction novels, Jean Auel's THE CLAN OF THE CAVE BEAR, Carl Sagan's BROCA'S BRAIN, several Isaac Asimov collections of science essays and two of his history books, ADVERTISING AGE and AD WEEK magazines, some programs on PBS, a couple of advertising textbooks I was examining for adoption in my class, and several other things I can't even remember now. This was pure research; I was reading and watching television for the sake of reading and watching about things I didn't know.

Relating all of the disparate facts and opinions in all of these sources led me to my opinions on stereotyping and pigeonholing as vital components of human thought, now a major element in my media criticism and advertising psychology classes. When I started I had no idea this pure research would lead where it did. I was just having fun.

Original Research

Original, or primary research is looking for information that nobody else has found. Observing people's response to advertising, how prison sentences influence crime rates, doing tests, observations, experiments, etc., are to discover something new.

Original research requires two things: 1) knowing what has already been discovered, having a background on the subject; and 2) formulating a method to find out what you want to know. To accomplish the first you indulge in secondary research (see below).

For the second, you decide how best to find the information you need to arrive at a conclusion. This method may be using focus groups, interviews, observations, expeditions, experiments, surveys, etc.

For example, you can decide to find out what the governmental system of the Hittite Empire was like on the basis of their communication system to determine how closely the empire could be governed by a central bureaucracy. The method to do this original research would probably require that you travel to the Middle East and examine such things as roads, systems of writing, courier systems without horses, archaeological evidence, actual extent of Hittite influence (commercial, military, laws, language, religion, etc.) and anything else you can think of and find any evidence for.

Secondary Research
Secondary research is finding out what others have discovered through original research and trying to reconcile conflicting viewpoints or conclusions, find new relationships between normally non-related research, and arrive at your own conclusion based on others' work. This is, of course, the usual course for college students.

An example from recent years was the relating of tectonic, geologic, biologic, paleontological, and astronomic research to each other. Relating facts from these researches led to the conclusion that the mass extinctions of 65 million years ago, including the dinosaurs, was the result of an asteroid or comet striking the earth in the North Atlantic at the site of Iceland. (For a full explanation see THE GREAT EXTINCTION by Michael Allaby and James Lovelock.) Later research based on the above has found a potential crater for the impact on the Yucatan Peninsula.

Secondary research should not be belittled simply because it is not original research. Fresh insights and viewpoints, based on a wide variety of facts gleaned from original research in many areas, has often been a source of new ideas. Even more, it has provided a clearer understanding of what the evidence means without the influence of the original researcher's prejudices and preconceptions.

Text 2

RESEARCH METHODOLOGY – AN INTRODUCTION

From: Research Methodology: Methods & Techniques
by C R Kothari (2004)

Reproduced by kind permission of the original publisher

MEANING OF RESEARCH

Research in common parlance refers to a search for knowledge. One can also define research as a scientific and systematic search for pertinent information on a specific topic. In fact, research is an art of scientific investigation. The Advanced Learner's Dictionary of Current English lays down the meaning of research as "a careful investigation or inquiry specially through search for new facts in any branch of knowledge." Redman and Mory define research as a "systematized effort to gain new knowledge." Some people consider research as a movement, a movement from the known to the unknown. It is actually a voyage of discovery. We all possess the vital instinct of inquisitiveness for, when the unknown confronts us, we wonder and our inquisitiveness makes us probe and attain full and fuller understanding of the unknown. This inquisitiveness is the mother of all knowledge and the method, which man employs for obtaining the knowledge of whatever the unknown, can be termed as research.

Research is an academic activity and as such the term should be used in a technical sense. According to Clifford Woody research comprises defining and redefining problems, formulating hypothesis or suggested solutions; collecting, organising and evaluating data; making deductions and reaching conclusions; and at last carefully testing the conclusions to determine whether they fit the formulating hypothesis. D. Slesinger and M. Stephenson in the Encyclopaedia of Social Sciences define research as "the manipulation of things, concepts or symbols for the purpose of generalising to extend, correct or verify knowledge, whether that knowledge aids in construction of theory or in the practice of an art." Research is, thus, an original contribution to the existing stock of knowledge making for its advancement. It is the pursuit of truth with the help of study, observation, comparison and experiment. In short, the search for knowledge through objective and systematic method of finding solution to a problem is research. The systematic approach concerning generalisation and the formulation of a theory is also research. As such the term 'research' refers to the systematic method consisting of enunciating the problem, formulating a hypothesis, collecting the facts or data, analysing the facts and reaching certain conclusions either in the form of solutions(s) towards the concerned problem or in certain generalisations for some theoretical formulation.

NOTES

OBJECTIVES OF RESEARCH

The purpose of research is to discover answers to questions through the application of scientific procedures. The main aim of research is to find out the truth which is hidden and which has not been discovered as yet. Though each research study has its own specific purpose, we may think of research objectives as falling into a number of following broad groupings:

1. To gain familiarity with a phenomenon or to achieve new insights into it (studies with this object in view are termed as exploratory or formulative research studies);
2. To portray accurately the characteristics of a particular individual, situation or a group (studies with this object in view are known as descriptive research studies);
3. To determine the frequency with which something occurs or with which it is associated with something else (studies with this object in view are known as diagnostic research studies);
4. To test a hypothesis of a causal relationship between variables (such studies are known as hypothesis-testing research studies).

MOTIVATION IN RESEARCH

What makes people [want] to undertake research? This is a question of fundamental importance. The possible motives for doing research may be either one or more of the following:

1. Desire to get a research degree along with its consequential benefits;
2. Desire to face the challenge in solving the unsolved problems, i.e., concern over practical problems initiates research;
3. Desire to get intellectual joy of doing some creative work;
4. Desire to be of service to society;
5. Desire to get respectability.

However, this is not an exhaustive list of factors motivating people to undertake research studies. Many more factors such as directives of government, employment conditions, curiosity about new things, desire to understand causal relationships, social thinking and awakening, and the like may as well motivate (or at times compel) people to perform research operations.

References
The Advanced Learner's Dictionary of Current English, Oxford, 1952, p. 1069.
L.V. Redman and A.V.H. Mory, The Romance of Research, 1923, p.10.
The Encyclopaedia of Social Sciences, Vol. IX, MacMillan, 1930.2 Research Methodology

Sample Presentations 3A & 3B
As You Watch

Now watch someone giving a presentation about each of the papers. Which presentation did you find more interesting or useful? Make notes in the space below.

Sample Presentation 3A

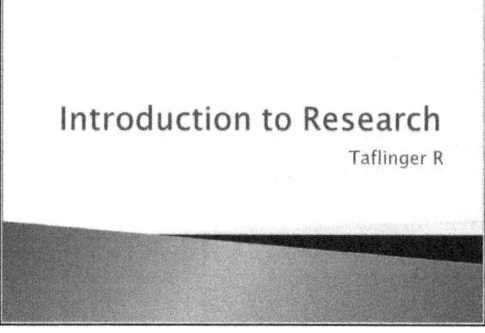

Sample Presentation 3B

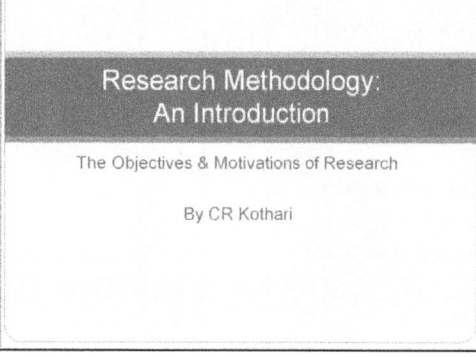

Notes

Presenting a paper

Learning Presentation 3.1

→ *Make Your Opinion Known*

Sometimes you might be asked to present a paper which will lead in to a seminar discussion on a topic. Based on the two presentations you have seen, what do you think is important in presenting a paper?

Watch Learning Presentation 2.1 and compare your ideas.

Language Focus

When you are presenting a paper it is important to show your stance. This means it is important to show what you think about what is said in the paper. You can show your opinion about something through the language you use. Think about the difference between these statements. What does the speaker think?

1. *Kothari says …*
2. *As Kothari rightly points out …*
3. *Perhaps the best definition is that given by Kothari which is …*
4. *Kothari makes the somewhat limited argument that …*
5. *Kothari builds on Taflinger's basic definition to say …*

Stance can be shown in different ways. Decide if the words below indicate a neutral, positive (+) or negative (-) stance.

Kothari	rightly somewhat dubiously convincingly rather weakly strongly	argues that …

| Kothari makes | the interesting / an unsupported / a bold / the surprising / the sophisticated | claim that … |

| Kothari | goes as far as to / breaks new ground to / has a lot of support to | suggest that … |

"Perhaps the best definition is the one that surprises us most."

Learning Presentation 3.2

You might also find that you are asked to present more than one paper. Watch the next Learning Presentation and make notes on the kind of things you need to remember when presenting more than one paper.

→ *Horizontal vs. Vertical*

Sample Presentation 3C

You are going to watch someone present the two papers reproduced at the start of this unit. Before you watch, discuss how you would present them and combine the information horziontally.

Now watch the presentation and decide how well the speaker presented the papers.

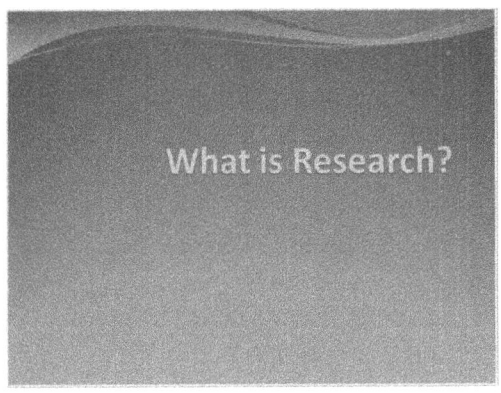 

Presentation Task 2

Read the papers below and choose one of them. Think about your reaction to what the paper says and what you think about the topic. Prepare a paper presentation and remember to end your presentation with questions for the audience to think about and talk about in the discussion which follows your presentation.

Make sure your language makes your stance clear throughout.

Text 3

Research Skills And The New Undergraduate
By B Quarton
From the *Journal of Instructional Psychology*
Vol. 30, No. 2, June 2003.

Reproduced by kind permission of the author

Abstract
Undergraduates are largely unaware of the myriad of information resources available to them in their university library; thus, many students rely on publicly accessible Internet sites for their research needs. This practice severely undermines the academic research efforts of undergraduates. Contrary to student opinion, the Internet does not encompass all the world's knowledge, nor is it likely to do so in the future. Students must learn to use specialized research tools and to approach all information sources with a critical eye. This article describes teaching strategies faculty in any discipline can use to guide their undergraduate students through the basic library research necessary for writing a solid research paper.

Introduction
University libraries have outstanding information resources available to their student populations--subject encyclopedias, monographs, periodical literature, dissertations--and they have powerful tools for accessing these materials--online catalogs, subscription databases, interlibrary loan services--but many college students are either unaware of these resources or they do not know how to use them. Because few universities require an assessment of information literacy as a condition of graduation, many students move from course to course with only a marginal understanding about how to use research tools and how to evaluate resources. At graduation, students lacking these information literacy skills are ill prepared to function in a technological and information-rich environment.

NOTES

For teaching faculty, information literacy is problematic. While it is widely agreed that information literacy is an essential component of higher education, it is unclear where it fits in the university curriculum: computer science classes, writing classes, or research methods courses. In fact, information literacy transcends course content and can be developed through course work in all disciplines. It is possible for individual faculty in any discipline to design assignments that provide the framework for a mastery of information literacy skills. This article identifies essential library resources for undergraduate students and, more important, presents teaching strategies that foster the acquisition of information literacy skills in the university classroom.

The Research Assignment
A typical undergraduate assignment involves choosing a topic in a discipline and writing a paper about it. Students are usually required to establish a premise and use literature from the field to corroborate their position. While this kind of assignment sounds straightforward, it is fraught with difficulties for undergraduates who lack information literacy skills: how does one focus a topic; how does one find literature pertaining to the topic; what is the "literature," and how does one distinguish it from other published materials?

Focusing the Topic
As beginning researchers, undergraduates usually do not know enough about specific disciplines to choose a focused avenue of research and to develop a manageable research question. There is, however, an important library tool that can be useful to students as they work to develop their research question: the subject encyclopaedia. While an encyclopaedia is a tertiary source (and therefore often overlooked by scholars), it is important to give it due respect as an excellent starting point for novices in the search for information. Unlike the general encyclopaedia, the subject encyclopaedia has longer articles that treat the topic in some depth while providing a context within the discipline. The articles present overviews, often including historical perspectives, theoretical frameworks, and issues of controversy, among other things, that help the new researcher find a foothold in the field. Of equal importance are the bibliographies that accompany the articles. These references direct the student to further reading, allowing them to explore the topic in a systematic way. The objective in using this library tool is for students to explore the topic in a general (non-threatening) way, from a reputable source, and hopefully to discover in themselves a curiosity that motivates them to examine the topic further.

Source: http://www.freepatentsonline.com/article/Journal-Instructional-Psychology/105478980.html

Text 4

Tips for Researching

Reproduced by kind permission of the British Library

Research is searching carefully, with a method, so that you can answer a question. It is wider than finding out a fact and more focused than reading widely around a subject.

These are some ideas to make your research process more interesting. They won't give you advanced skills in specialist subjects but they could be inspiring if you are starting a research project, if you haven't done much research in your subject or if you need a fresh angle.

The most effective researchers:

- take time to plan
- find a question that is both challenging and possible, both open and focused
- check their research doesn't beg a question*
- explore many kinds of sources, not just textbooks
- learn how to speed-read
- get quickly to relevant information
- think analytically and imaginatively about what they find
- store their notes in efficient and interesting ways
- collaborate with others and take on other people's views
- present their final ideas in inspiring and effective ways
- use what they find to solve a problem or make a difference

*begging a question means that the process of questioning is lacking a key piece of information or a key concept.

Make a map
At the start of a project, when you aren't sure where to draw the boundaries, get a huge sheet of paper and make a map or diagram of all of your questions, associations, sources and leads. Mark your most compelling thoughts in a strong colour. Mark the main links to those ideas in that colour too. Don't throw out the weaker or isolated thoughts, but this map will help you know their place. You could make another map later in the project when you feel there is too much information.

Archive your questions
It is common to archive quotes and extracts but we forget to keep a record of our questions. Record who originally asked the question and leave a space by each one to record answers or places to look for answers. Highlight the questions that you find most challenging, the ones that wake you up. Archiving questions will encourage you to articulate them well. If you form your thoughts as questions, it will help you realise what you need to research. (Of course, some questions will be very specific which might not be interesting to archive separately.)

Switch mode
Refresh yourself by exploring different types of source. If you've been reading history, find out about Sound Archives so that you can listen to some oral history. If you've been studying art, break out by exploring poetry or music that relates to the period or place. How you switch depends on what you normally do.

Walkabout
Find a way of using a walk to gather information for your research. Go with other people so you can talk. Look at buildings, get on a train out of town, do a survey, take photos and sketches, watch people, collect samples. Make a creative record of the walk – use mobile phone cameras, i-pods, GPS waypoints, survey forms, a long scroll of paper or notebooks. Finish the day reviewing your findings over refreshments.

Blog it
If you're confident to share your research in its raw ongoing state with others, you could post summaries of your findings and questions on a weblog. This could be a group or individual blog. You could ask for site visitors to suggest further reading, new research methods or to answer your questions.

Use del.icio.us
This is free online service that lets you store and organise everything you find and like on the web. For each page you store, you can write comments and tag them with keywords. You can also see how many other people like that page and see their comments on it. If you cut and paste web content into your research notes and essays, but forget to note where it came from, del.icio.us helps you keep track.

Talk it over
If you have to write an article or essay, but you can't get started with writing or there isn't enough published information, it helps to interview someone else who is interested or informed on the subject. Ask them questions you really want the answers to. Make it a real conversation. Make sure you record it.

Read at speed

If you want to practice speed-reading, be competitive about it. Set timed challenges with a friend or a group. Read an article or chapter at the same time. When you've finished, each write down the three most interesting things in the piece. Look on the web for tips on speed reading.

In the margins

Sometimes research is effective if it is analysing or interpreting one book, article, theory, design, poem or work of art. Buy a copy of the book or photocopy the document you need. Have absolutely no qualms about writing and drawing all over it. Devise a system for yourself, e.g. with colours or symbols to mark words you don't understand, references to follow up, questions, opinions and so on. Fill it with post-its and book-marks. Keep it with you. (Please remember not to write in library books!)

Get real

Make a product, or think about an application, even if your project doesn't require one. If you feel that your research is too abstract or you're not motivated enough, think about how you could apply it or explain it to others. Could it lead to a new invention? Could you write a book with this? Could you make money from it? What would it be like if it was translated into a TV programme or an exhibition? How might you use it to influence an organisation to change its practices?

Source: http://www.bl.uk/learning/cresearch/skills/ideas1/ideas.html

- Make a map
- Switch mode
- Talk it over
- Get real

Project Introduction – Approaching A Topic

At the end of this course you are going to give a 20 minute presentation on the subject of smartphones. This will be an opportunity for you to prepare a presentation based on whichever aspect of smartphones you want to discuss. Read the following introduction about smartphones and then brainstorm which aspects of smartphones you would be interested in presenting on, which could be anything from marketing strategies, design features, social impact or economic implications. Remember, the point of the presentation will be to engage your audience and tell them something interesting about smartphones they may not already know.

Smartphones

A smartphone is a phone which combines the features of a traditional phone with additional computing power. Rather than being simply used for making calls and sending texts, smartphones can access the internet and run applications. As outlined by Charlesworth (2009), smartphones developed as a combination of the features of a mobile phone and a PDA (Personal Digital Assistant). Since their initial introduction into the phone market, the computing power of smartphones has grown rapidly – the modern smartphone having more computing power than the most powerful computer in the world had in 1985 (Arthur, 2011). This increased power means smartphones are able to do much more than just connect us to the internet – they can help people monitor their health (Lam, 2009), conduct business (Carayannis & Clark, 2011) and have access to education (Herrington, 2008). With the dramatic rise in the sales of smartphones (Charlesworth, 2009, Arthur, 2011), there has been fierce competition between both handset makers and, perhaps more importantly, operating systems (Lin, 2009). While Apple still dominates the smartphone market, particularly at the top end of the market, Samsung have gained significant market share with its wider range of handsets (Gartner Inc, 2012), leading to bitter legal battles between the two companies (Carrier, 2012).

These legal disputes range from issues of design to technical design features. Regardless of the outcome, however, it is clear that smartphones will continue to have an increasingly important impact on how people live day to day and could be responsible for lifting people out of poverty (Prasad, K, 2012).

References

Arthur, C (2011) How the Smartphone is Killing the PC. The Guardian Newspaper (online) 5th June 2011. Available at http://www.guardian.co.uk/technology/2011/jun/05/smartphones-killing-pc (accessed October 2012)

Carayannis, E & Clark, S (2011) Do Smartphones Make for Smarter Business? The Smartphone CEO Study. *Journal of the Knowledge Economy*, Vol 2, No. (2011), 201-233

Carrier, M (2012) A Roadmap to the Smartphone Patent Wars and FRAND Licensing. *CPI Antitrust Chronicle*. Vol. 2, April 2012

Charlesworth, A (2009) The Ascent of Smartphone. Available online at http://ieeexplore.ieee.org/stamp/stamp.jsp?tp=&arnumber=4913985 (accessed October 2012)

Gartner Inc (2012) *Gartner Says Worldwide Smartphone Sales Soared in Fourth Quarter of 2011 With 47 Per Cent Growth* [Press Release] Available at http://www.pressebox.de/attachment/447933/Mobile+Devices+4Q11+FINAL+EMEA+version.pdf (accessed Oct 2012)

Herrington, A (2008) Adult educators' authentic use of smartphones to create digital teaching resources. Available online at http://www.ascilite.org.au/conferences/melbourne08/procs/herrington-a.pdf (accessed October 2012)

Lam, S (2009) A smartphone-centric platform for personal health monitoring using wireless wearable biosensors. Available online at http://ieeexplore.ieee.org/xpls/abs_all.jsp?arnumber=5397628 (accessed October 2012)

Lin, F (2009) Operating System Battle in the Ecosystem of Smartphone Industry. Available online at http://ieeexplore.ieee.org/xpls/abs_all.jsp?arnumber=5175193 (accessed October 2012)

Prasad, K (2012) Mobile Communication for Sustainable Development: Change and Challenges in South Asia. Available online at http://kau.diva-portal.org/smash/get/diva2:472880/FULLTEXT01#page=178 (accessed October 2012)

Review of SP 3A, 3B & 3C

These presentations are in-class presentations of a paper or papers the students have read and are meant to start a class discussion.

Organising language 4

Good morning everybody. Today I'm here to talk about …

Today we're here to talk about …

I'm here today to talk about … which is an article by …

The purpose of my presentation today is to …

To begin with …

I'd like to start by …

So to finish my presentation I would like to …

Talking about a paper

In that paper …

According to Taflinger, …

He goes on to discuss …

The final thing that he discusses in the paper is …

He gives us … and also outlines …

The article gives us an idea about …

At the outset of the paper …

He talks about …

He specifies …

Later in the paper he talks about …

The final reason he gives …

He also went on to talk in more detail about …

The two papers looked at …

We can look at the two papers and we can see …

Reacting to a paper

The way he talked about … made me think …

I think that's the one that's most interesting and relevant …

So for me …

Particularly …

> **Comment**
>
> *3A is not a very successful discussion of a paper. The presenter just repeats the main information with no analysis, interpretation or reaction.*
>
> *3B is better; the presenter still talks about the main information but is more selective, giving more attention to the ideas he found more interesting. There is also an attempt to see how the information in the paper applies to students generally.*
>
> *In 3C the presenter highlights how ideas in the two papers can be connected, and also gives some evaluation of what the information means.*

Unit 4
Elevator Pitch Poster Presentations

Unit 4 Elevator Pitch Poster Presentations

Unit Aims

When you are presenting, you might have to give a group presentation. You might also have to give something called an elevator pitch poster presentation. In this kind of presentation you have 30 seconds to give your presentation and you can use a poster as a visual aid to help.

- How should a group of people work together to produce a presentation?
- What are some of the basic principles of designing effective visual aids?
- How can you give an effective presentation in 30 seconds?

At the end of the unit, return to these questions and see how much your answers may have changed or developed.

Working in groups

During your studies you will often be asked to work in a group and it's important to know some principles of good teamwork. Teams do not just work well by accident.

In groups discuss what the following things mean in relation to teamwork. Think back to any teams you worked in and come up with suggestions of what makes a successful team and what problems people can face in group-work tasks.

Sample Presentation 4A

You're now going to watch a presentation about working in teams. Make a note of anything you find interesting.

As you watch, pay attention to the slides and think about what makes visual aids effective when giving a presentation.

Presentation Task 3

You are going to form a team with some other students. Together you are going to:

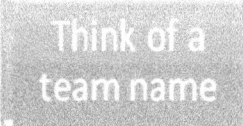

When you have finished you are going to present your team to the class, introducing your group and explaining the meaning behind your name, flag and motto.

When you have finished the presentation, think about these questions:

- Did the team finish the task satisfactorily?
- What role do you think you played in the team?
- Who was the team leader and did they lead the team well?
- What role do the others think you played in the team?
- Did the team have the right balance of roles?

Learning Presentation 4.1

→ *Everyone Has A Role*

You've been thinking about teamwork and how groups can work successfully. You've also just developed a group presentation.

Watch the next Learning Presentation and make notes about things to consider in a group presentation.

Managing Group Presentations

Language Focus

Diplomatic Language
When you are working with other people, you have to be diplomatic (polite). In an academic presentation you should also avoid strong or emotional language. Look at the phrases below and think of alternative ways of saying the same thing in a diplomatic way.

You're wrong.	
I don't agree with you.	
That's a stupid thing to say.	
I don't care.	
Shut up. I want to say something.	

Poster presentations

You won't always have PowerPoint available to support your presentation and sometimes presentation software may not be the best choice. You might use a poster instead. Look at the following three posters about helping the environment and decide what makes an effective poster. Make notes in the box below.

Tips for good posters

Learning Presentation 4.2

→ *Making An Impact*

Watch the Learning Presentation about designing posters and add to your notes on makes an effective poster.

Elevator pitch presentations

You might use a poster to support something called an elevator pitch presentation. The idea behind an elevator pitch presentation is to get your message across in 30 seconds – the time you might have to sell an idea to a busy executive as your ride together in an elevator. To do this well, your presentation has to be very focused and have a single, clear message.

Presentation Task 4

Work with your group and decide how you would present this poster about teamwork. The purpose of the presentation is to inform a group of students new to university about the value of teamwork.

Decide what your message is going to be and prepare a 30 second group presentation. Consider who will present and what the other members of the group will be doing during the presentation.

As you watch other groups presenting the same poster, decide which group did it most effectively. What made their presentation work so well?

Overcoming nerves

If you get nervous before giving a presentation, don't worry - it can be controlled. Try this:

1. Take a long slow breath, thinking 'I'm ready for this.'
2. Breathe out slowly, thinking 'The audience is going to enjoy this.'
3. Take another long slow breath, thinking '**I'm** going to enjoy this.'
4. Breathe out slowly, thinking 'This is going to go well.'

If you control your breathing, you go a long way towards controlling your nerves. Smile, and you're ready to begin.

Language Focus

To Script or Not to Script
Some students write a script when they have to prepare a presentation, which they then learn and deliver. A problem with scripting is that a scripted presentation might not sound natural and there are also some things that work well on paper that don't work as well when delivered orally. Also, because a script is fixed, it can cause trouble if you encounter the unexpected, for example, if a member of the audience asks a question or if you forget a particular phrase.

Rather than scripting, it's a better idea to have an outline of your presentation and be clear on the steps in your argument. You should also think about different ways of making the same point so if you do forget something, you have an alternative ready.

Using Notecards
In a longer presentation it might be a good idea to use notecards to remind you of the steps you are going to make in your presentation. If you do use notecards, they should

- fit comfortably in your hand
- be numbered clearly so they don't get mixed up
- use a large font size you can read easily
- use bullet points rather than sentences
- have one main topic per card
- only contain key information

While flexibility is a good thing in a longer presentation, in an elevator pitch presentation it is usually a good idea to have a script. Since you have so little time, you have to make sure every word is necessary and adds to your message.

Learning Presentation 4.3

Elevated Pitch Presentations

→ *Making A Point in 30 Seconds or Less*

This type of presentation is sometimes referred to as an *elevated* pitch presentation. This alternative name suggests that the impact is raised to a higher level because of the short time available. Watch the Learning Presentation and make notes on the advice given.

Based on the advice you have just listened to, and what you thought watching other groups present, revise your poster presentation and deliver it again.

Presentation Task 5

You are now going prepare an elevator pitch poster presentation with your group and the purpose of the presentation is to explain what you think makes a good leader. Design a poster and a thirty-second pitch.

Review of SP 4A – Managing Teamwork

This is an informative presentation which gives the audience an overview of teamwork and suggests how teams could work effectively.

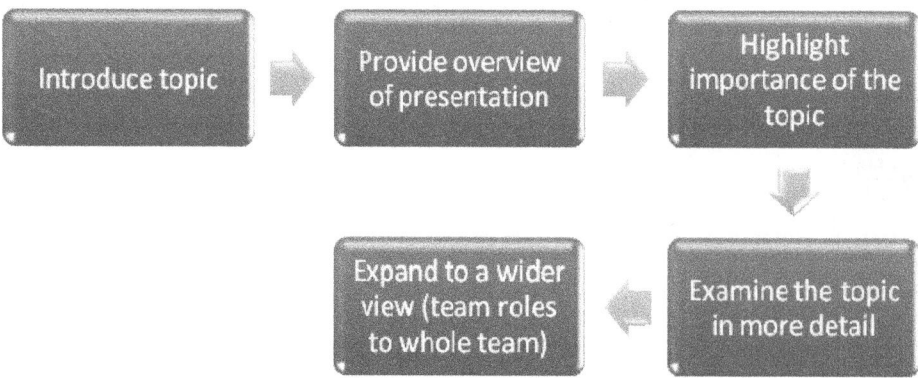

Outlining structure

Good afternoon ladies and gentlemen. Thank you for coming along today.

My name is ... and I'm here to talk to you about ...

Before I get started, I'd like to give you a quick overview of what we'll be discussing today.

I'm going to start out by thinking about ...

Then we're going to move on to think about ...

We're going to think about ...

And finally, I'm going to think about ...

So, to begin with, let's think about ...

Notice the presenter relies too much on 'think about'.

Rhetorical questions

A rhetorical question is a question you do not expect the audience to answer but which you ask so they think about a particular thing.

So, at university, what are the expectations of teams? When you're given a group task, what do your lecturers expect? Well, they expect that ...

Introducing background

Now in order to understand ... I'd like to tell you a little ...

Directing the audience's attention

So, if we look at the slide ...

Explaining difficult terminology

The next ... is something called .... Now, that may not be clear, but what it means is ...

The final role identified by Belbin is the specialist. Now, a specialist is someone who ...

Emphasising points

The important thing to remember is ...

Comment

This presentation develops quite logically – thinking about individuals in teams before moving on to the operation of the team as a whole. Perhaps, however, the leadership issue could have been handled at a different stage in the presentation so that the presentation keeps moving forward. As it stands, the presentation discusses roles, teams and then roles again, which is a little circular. Perhaps a better organisation would have been as shown below. In this way the presentation would have moved from the basic (viewing team roles as leader or member) to complex (considered a wider range of roles) before looking at the issue more widely (how teams work).

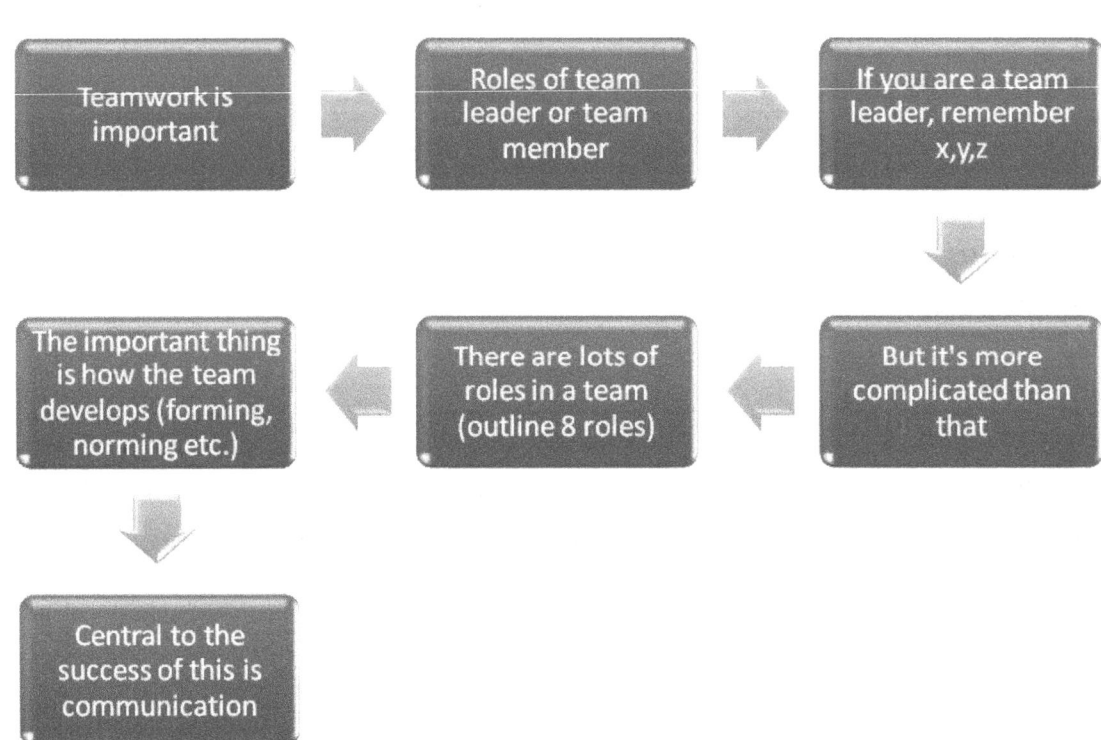

Unit 5
Persuasive Presentations

Unit 5 Persuasive Presentations

Unit Aims

Whenever you give a presentation, you need to be thinking about the effect you have on your audience and at the end of your presentation you will probably want your audience to agree with your position.

- How can you try to make people agree with you during a presentation?
- What do you know about different ways of collecting information for research?
- How can you make language persuasive?

At the end of the unit, return to these questions and see how much your answers may have changed or developed.

Sample Presentation 5A

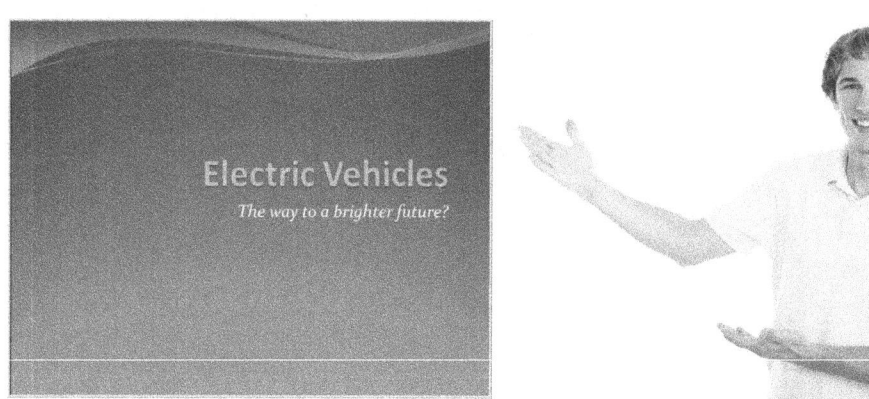

When we were thinking about what made a presentation academic in Unit 2, we watched three different presentations. Re-watch the second presentation and in the space below make a note of how the speaker tries to push the audience to agree with his position that electric cars are not a good option. Think about the presentation organisation, content, delivery and language.

Notes

Language Focus

Persuasive Language
There are different techniques we can use to be persuasive in our language.

Repetition	During the presentation, the speaker stressed how electric cars let Bob and Sue down, let the environment down and let us all down. This repetition of something, particularly repeating it three times, can be very powerful.
Using Intensifiers	An intensifier is something which makes language stronger : • *This is a problem.* • *This is a **serious** problem.* • *This is a **very serious** problem.* • *This is an **extremely serious** problem.*
Inclusive language	During the presentation, the speaker talked about 'us' and 'them'. 'We' and 'us' brings people together, 'they' and 'them' creates distance. You are more likely to agree with a group you are a part of.
Personalisation	Feelings are powerful – if you share how you feel about something with your audience, if you use 'I' and 'you', your feelings can affect the audience's feelings.
Possibility	If you say something is true, you have to prove it. If you say something *'could be true'* or *'might be true'*, the amount of proof you need to give is not as great. This means you can emphasise things more. Compare: • *The use of petrol powered cars is affecting the environment.* with • *The use of petrol powered cars **may well** result in disastrous environmental damage.*
Short sentences	Short sentences, if used well, can make a big impact. You don't want to overuse short sentences, but they can be a very useful tool. • *There are many problems caused by electric cars. But I'm not going to waste your time telling you about all of them. No. I'm going to tell you about the most important. Pollution.*
Emotive language	Emotive language is language which has an effect on people's emotions. It can be the stronger way of saying the same thing. Compare • *Electric batteries are **difficult** to dispose of cleanly.* with • *Electric batteries are **poisoning** the earth and killing the planet.* or • *Electric cars are **a bad idea**.* with • *Electric cars would be **a tragedy for the planet**.*

Presentation Task 6

Choose one of the topics below and work with a partner to decide if it is a good idea or not. Work with a partner and decide what you would say to persuade someone to accept your opinion. You will have five minutes of presentation time, including questions, to make your case.

Studying overseas   *Capital punishment*   *Eating meat*

Now present your idea to the class. At the end of the presentation, see how many people agree with you.

Research methods

You are going to watch another presentation during which the presenter will recommend a research methodology. Before you watch, read the following introductory text and decide what the advantages and disadvantages of qualitative and quantitative research methods may be.

Qualitative and Quantitative Research Methods

In Unit 3 we looked at why people do research at university – to build knowledge to help answer questions. There are lots of different types of research methods, different ways of finding out information. The different types of research methodologies can be divided into two main types, quantitative and qualitative.

Quantitative research includes questionnaires or surveys where the researcher gives a large group of people a list of closed questions (yes/no questions, or questions with a scale answer, e.g. 1 = agree fully, 5 = disagree fully) and is able to gather data which can result in statistics, e.g. "52% of people think electric cars are a good idea". Qualitative research methods include techniques like interviews or focus groups, where people have the opportunity to express their ideas on a topic, so we might learn *why* those people think electric cars are a good idea.

One of the main differences between quantitative and qualitative research methods is that quantitative methods usually entail a bigger sample; you can send 1,000 people a questionnaire online much more quickly and easily than you could interview 1,000 people.

Sample Presentation 5B

Presentation 5A tried to be persuasive, but when we looked at it in Unit 2 we decided it was not an academic presentation. What do you think are the features of a persuasive *academic* presentation? After discussing your ideas, watch the second Sample Presentation and see how closely it matches what you thought a persuasive academic presentation would be.

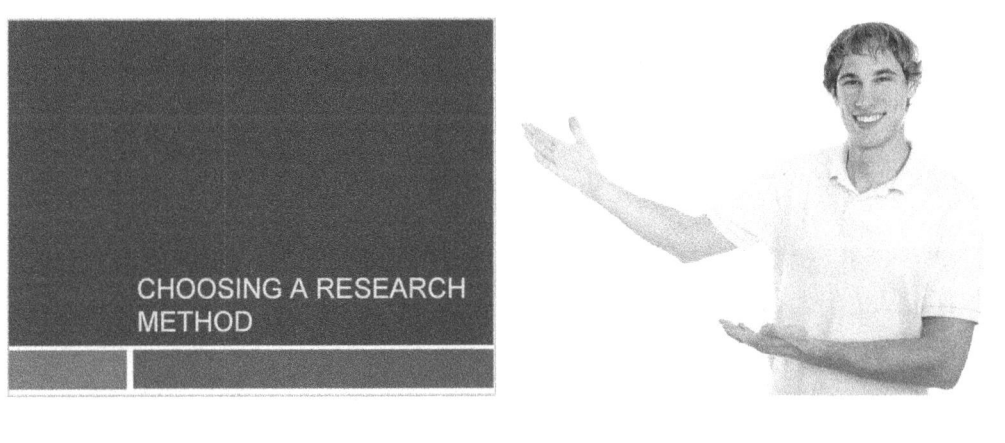

Learning Presentation 5.1

→ *Substance Over Style*

Based on your discussions and your ideas from watching the two sample persuasive presentations, you should have a good idea of what makes a good persuasive academic presentation. Watch the Learning Presentation to check your ideas.

Presentation Task 7

Now you are going to prepare a presentation about a type of research such as an interview, focus group or survey. The title of your presentation is

'Why xxx is the most valuable form of research'

The purpose of your presentation is to persuade your audience that your chosen research methodology is the best one.

You could structure your presentation like this

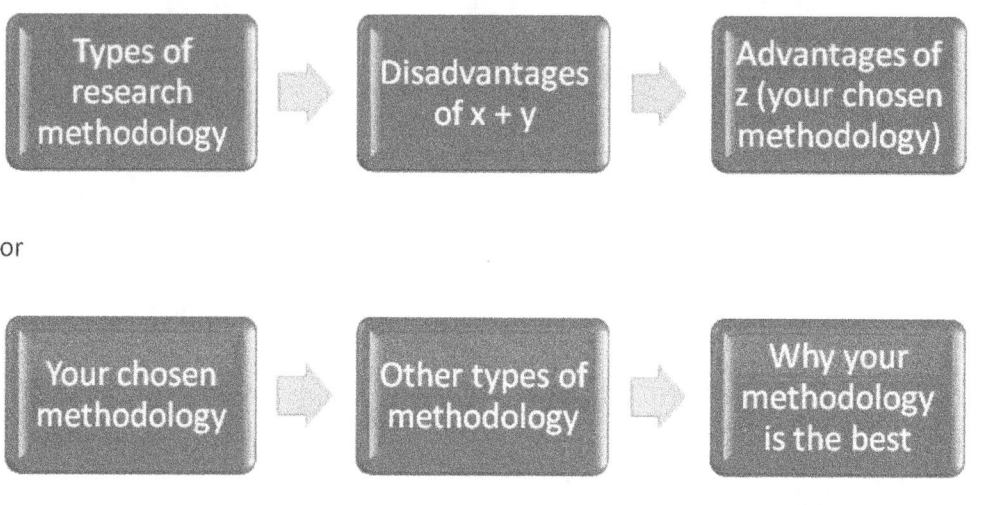

or

Remember, it is not just your opinion which matters. You will have to get some evidence to support your argument and make it clear to your audience where that evidence comes from.

Review of SP 5B – Choosing A Research Method

This is a presentation which is trying to persuade the audience towards the position that mixed methodologies are the most appropriate.

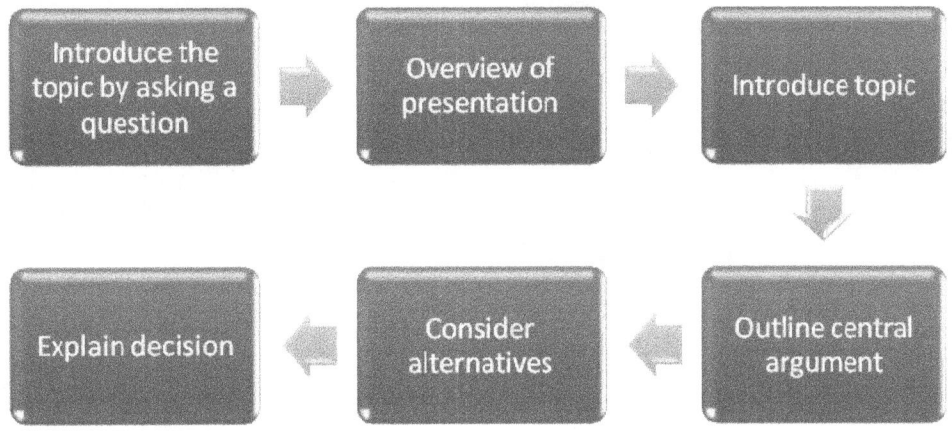

Opening with a question

You could open your presentation with a question but be very careful if you do. If you don't get the answer you hope for or expect, it could damage your entire presentation.

Before I get started, I'd like to ask …
And how many of you would agree …

Referring to sources

Based on my reading of …
According to …

Presenting your position

My argument today is …
I think the most obvious reason …
Importantly, I think …
However, despite those weaknesses, I do think …

Providing examples

It involves things like …
Things like …

Discussing advantages

The advantages of ... are ...

The advantages of this would be...

Discussing disadvantages

The disadvantages, however, are ...

And perhaps it doesn't ...

There could also be a lack of ...

However, there are some issues with ...

"On balance, it seems that the advantages outweigh the disadvantages."

Dealing with Questions 1

Question 1 – why aren't methods mixed?
For the first question the presenter should have taken a moment to think. He started to answer the question immediately and this led to having to rephrase the start of the answer.

I think it would be a question of the … erm … it makes it more complicated.

One of the strengths of the answer is that it goes back to sources rather than being pure opinion.

In the reading that I was doing about …

Question 2 – room for error in research
The presenter seems more confident of this answer and gives an extended response which directly answers the question asked.

Acknowledging a point

I suppose you could say that.

Question 3 – clarification of the problem of having more data
This is a question that could have been avoided by being clearer in the body of the presentation. When preparing a presentation, think about questions your audience may ask and see if there is a way of answering them in advance in the body of your presentation.

Clarifying a point

What I meant by that was…

Comment

On the whole, this is a successful, persuasive academic presentation. The presenter uses evidence from sources to support a clear position. It would strengthen the argument to have more than one source supporting each point and it would also help to have support from a source for mixed methodology. When talking about the advantages and disadvantages of mixed methodologies, the presenter is basing things more on personal opinion than directly on support from a source or evidence. However, it is clear the presenter is informed about different types of research and the conclusions are based on consideration of the advantages and disadvantages of those methods.

The presenter also deals with the questions reasonably well, although taking time to consider an answer rather than jumping straight in would be more effective. It is also a good idea to ask if you have answered the question to the questioner's satisfaction, particularly if you have to give quite a long answer.

Unit 6
Presenting Progress

Unit 6 Seminar Presentations 2 - Presenting Progress

Unit Aims

When you are working on a project, part way through the process you might be asked to give a presentation to update people on what you have been doing.

- What are the important things to cover in a progress presentation?
- What do you need to think about when using presentation software such as PowerPoint?
- What language can you use to talk about the past and future?

At the end of the unit, return to these questions and see how much your answers may have changed or developed.

An effective presentation is built on good planning. At the very beginning, once you know what your presentation is about and who the audience is, you need to start planning. You have been working on a presentation about smartphones. If you had to give a progress presentation about your smartphone project, what information would you include and how would you organise it? Make a plan of your presentation below.

Progress Presentation Outline

Compare your plan with other students. Did you approach the presentation in the same way?

Learning Presentation 6.1

→ *Two Approaches*

The way you structure a progress presentation may change, depending on how well your project is going. Watch the Learning Presentation and then look back at your progress presentation plan – is it based on the project going well or badly?

Language Focus

Past and Future
When you're giving a progress presentation you will be talking about the past (what you have done so far) and the future (what you are going to do next).

Talking About The Past
Look at the sentences below and put the verbs in the appropriate past tense. Today is November 12th.

1. My plan ……………….. (be) to start with data collection at the beginning of October.

2. I ……………….. (hope) to complete this by the end of the month but there ……………….. (be) a delay as people ……………….. (be) too busy to take part in my interviews.

3. However, while I ……………….. (wait) to gather the data I was also able to read more about interview techniques.

4. This meant by the time I ……………….. (start) the interviews I ……………….. (can) approach them with confidence.

Talking About The Future
Look at the sentences below and put the verbs in the appropriate future form.

1. Now that I have the data, the next stage is to start data analysis. The first stage .... (be) to listen to the interview recordings and take notes.
2. After that I .... (have to) see what the common features are.
3. I hope I .... (complete) the data analysis by the end of November.
4. Then I .... (able to) move on to the discussion part of my paper.

Talking About Plans
When you are talking about your plans you will be talking about things you

   hope   intend   plan   expect   want   anticipate

Learning Presentation 6.2

→ *Helping The Audience Follow Your Message*

When you are planning your presentation, you may decide to use, or be told you have to use, some presentation software to support your presentation. Based on what was discussed about poster design and the presentations you have seen, what do you think makes visual aids effective? Watch the Learning Presentation and make a note of any additional ideas.

Dealing with Questions 2

A presentation is just a beginning. It is the start of a conversation and a successful presentation should encourage the audience to ask questions. If they ask questions, it means they are interested in what you had to say and want to know more.

Strategies for Dealing with Questions
Questions can be the most complicated part of a presentation as it is the part where you may lose control because you don't know in advance what the audience will ask. There are different strategies for dealing with questions, particularly when you are not sure of the answer.

Discuss the following strategies with a partner – which do you think are the best to use?

	Strategy	Good idea?
Panic	You don't understand the question so talk about anything connected to your presentation.	
Repetition	Go back and repeat the part of your presentation connected to the question.	
Clarification	Ask the questioner to rephrase the question, or rephrase it yourself to make sure you understand what they are asking.	
Reflection	Ask the questioner what they think.	
Deflection	Explain that isn't part of your presentation.	
Admission	If you don't know the answer, say you don't know.	

Sample Presentations 6A

Watch the sample progress presentation and see how well the presenter deals with the questions. What different strategies does the presenter use when they have a problem with a question?

Do you think the presenter deals with the questions well?

"I'm glad you asked that question."

Project Review – Giving A Progress Presentation

Presentation Task 8

You have been working on a project about smartphones. You are going to give a presentation to the class about how it is going.

Look back at the plan you made at the start of this unit. Is there anything you would change in it? Outline the revised presentation in the space below. Also consider whether you are going to use presentation software to support your presentation. If so, which software will you use and how will you use it? For example, how many slides will you need and what will be the purpose of each one?

Outline of revised presentation

Review of SP 6A – Are Smartphones Destroying Language?

This is a progress presentation which has a basic problem in terms of the project not being very organised. The presentation itself is fine but the issue comes from a question about the methodology of the project.

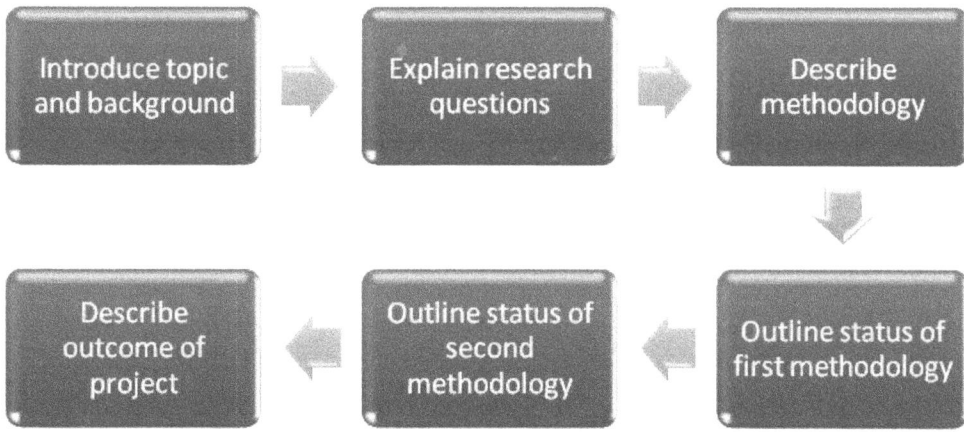

85

Explaining how your project started

What led me to this was ...

The thing that caught my attention ...

I came across another very interesting report ...

That is what led me into this project.

Describing research

The vast majority ...

I came across (a paper) which revealed ...

The argument of this (paper) ...

Within that same report, they found that ...

Explaining methodology

I'm first of all going to be ...

In that survey I'll be trying to find out ...

Then I'll be doing some analysis ...

I want to conduct ...

I've put together a survey, which is divided into two main sections ...

The intention is to send this ...

In terms of the analysis, ...

The reason I'd like to look at ...

I assume that ...

Within that analysis I'm going to be looking for ...

Describing outcomes

The outcome of my project should be that we will have a clear picture of ...

We will also have a clear picture of ...

We'll also have an evaluation of ...

Dealing with Questions 3

This presenter runs into trouble in the question stage of the presentation because the audience cannot understand how he intends to conduct part of his project. When you are working on a project it is important to remember that things that seem clear to you must be equally clear to your audience.

Question 1 – validity of source
The presenter doesn't seem too clear about where the sources came from – you should always be prepared to say what your sources are so the audience can see how powerful they are. This is also something that needs to be highlighted in the body of the presentation.

Question 2 – age of source
The question of the age of a source is interesting. However, the presenter does a reasonable job of referring to a later source to show how the information is still relevant. It was also good to remind the audience that the first part of the project would see if texting was still relevant.

Question 3 – other factors which could contribute to language ability
This is the question where the problems in the proposed methodology begin to become clear. The presenter's logic is quite convincing but the questioner still has questions. The follow up question presses the same point and this question is not dealt with particularly well.

Question 4 – how to identify the effect of texting
The presenter tries to avoid this question entirely and gives a very empty response to the follow-up question.

Question 5 – clarification of high and low frequency texters
The presenter has a clear answer to this question but this information might have been better included in the body of the presentation. Define terms clearly, particularly those you generate yourself.

Question 6 – balance of respondents
This question is answered quite clearly, but it is not clear the presenter had actually thought about this aspect of their study before.

Question 7 – size of sample size
The presenter demonstrates they have put some thought into the methodology in terms of sample size.

Question 8 – analysis of writing

The presenter asks for clarification of this question *"How do you mean?"* but this should be done more professionally.
There isn't a really clear answer to this
question. The methodology of analysis should be much clearer.

The presenter also uses language which would make the audience lose confidence that they knew what they were doing:

I guess I'm trying to find out

Comment

Although delivered reasonably well, this is not a particularly successful presentation as what is being presented is not well considered. A successful academic presentation depends on sound content so make sure you are very clear what you are presenting.

The first methodology is clear and seems reasonable. However, the second lacks clarity in terms of how the analysis will be carried out.

The presenter also needed more rehearsal as there is a lot of hesitation and overuse of fillers like 'erm' and 'uhm'.

Unit 7
Problem/Solution Presentations

Unit 7   Problem/Solution Presentations

Unit Aims

You might be asked to give a presentation where you have to analyse a problem and suggest solutions or give recommendations.

- How many different ways could you organise information in a problem/solution presentation?
- What is plagiarism, and how can you avoid it?
- What language can you use to talk about possibility?

At the end of the unit, return to these questions and see how much your answers may have changed or developed.

You just discussed plagiarism. Look at the text below and make a note of what you learn.

What is Plagiarism?
By Peter Levrai (2012)

Plagiarism is a serious concern in universities. If you submit a piece of work which is plagiarised then you could face very serious consequences – from failing the assignment to losing your place at university. Most basically, plagiarism means using someone else's words or ideas in an essay or presentation, without telling the reader where the information came from.

It can be quite easy to plagiarise without realising, as plagiarism is more than copying the exact words from a text. Plagiarism also includes using the same sentence structure and replacing words with synonyms, for example:

Original Text
Plagiarism is a very serious offence in academic writing.

Plagiarised Text
Plagiarism is an extremely serious offence in academic writing.

Similarly, making small changes to sentence structure (e.g. turning active sentences into passive sentences) but keeping a lot of the same vocabulary is also considered plagiarism.

> **Original Text**
> Students who plagiarise suffer severe consequences.
>
> **Plagiarised Text**
> Severe consequences are suffered by students who plagiarise.
>
> However, your writing and presentations are expected to be based on information from sources so you will be discussing other people's ideas. The important thing is that you give a citation (author, date) to show your reader where the information came from and that you are using the ideas rather than the language.
>
> If you use the exact words from the text, you have to use quotation marks (" ") and put the page number the quote came from in the citation, e.g. (Levrai, 2012:46). There should be a limit to the amount of quotations you use as in an essay your lecturers want to see your own words. Rather than using a lot of quotations, it is better to paraphrase, to discuss the ideas from the source in your own words and again give a citation (author surname, date of publication). By paraphrasing you are showing you understand what the source is talking about and by citing you are telling the reader where they can go and check your information.

Look at the two texts below, which are based on the first paragraph of the passage above, and discuss with a partner in what ways the first text is guilty of plagiarism and how the second text avoids plagiarising. Make notes in the box below.

> **Text 1**
> Plagiarism can be a major problem at universities. Students who hand in plagiarised work can face very serious consequences. They might fail the assignment or even be dismissed from university. Plagiarism is when a writer uses someone else's words or ideas in a piece of work but does not tell the reader where the information came from.

Text 2

As Levrai (2012) points out, plagiarism is a serious issue. At university, students have to write essays based on other sources but it is important when they do so that they specify in their essays which sources the ideas come from. Failure to do so would lay them open to a charge of plagiarism, which could result in disciplinary action, extending from failing their assignment to being dismissed from university entirely.

Tips For Avoiding Plagiarism

If you were going to give a problem/solution presentation called **'Avoiding Plagiarism'**, how would you organise it?

Sample Presentation 7A

Watch the Sample Presentation and see how the presenter has structured it. Do they take the steps you thought they would? As you watch, add to your list of tips for avoiding plagiarism if the presenter gives a suggestion you had not already considered.

Citing and referencing

To avoid plagiarism you are going to have to cite and provide a reference list. You should check with your lecturers which style of referencing they require as there are several different types. The presentations and texts in this course use the Harvard Style. A very useful guide to the Harvard Referencing style can be found on the website given below:

http://libweb.anglia.ac.uk/referencing/harvard.htm

Look back at Sample Presentations 4A and 5A and compare how they use citations on slides and in their reference lists. Which one follows the Harvard Style correctly?

Learning Presentation 7.1

 → *Cause and Effect*

When you are giving a problem/solution presentation, there are different ways you can structure it. Watch the Learning Presentation and then discuss why you might choose to use one structure rather than another. Which do you think might be more effective?

Presentation Task 9

In Unit 4 we briefly looked at the issue of scripting a presentation. Having learnt a lot more about presenting since then, you are now going to prepare a short presentation about

Students presenting from a memorised script

For the purpose of this presentation, full scripting and memorisation are a problem. You have to suggest solutions in the course of your presentation.

Presentation planning

Think about the issue → Read the following texts → Identify causes and effects → Come up with solutions

Text 1

A presentation is an opportunity to see how well a student understands a subject. Since there is the opportunity to ask questions at the end of a presentation it is possible to see how well read and well informed they are. Reading from a memorised script gives the impression that the student doesn't really understand the topic of the presentation and that is something that can become very clear during the questions when they no longer have the script to rely on.

(Mason, 2004)

Text 2

Giving a presentation can be very intimidating – many people are nervous when it comes to any kind of public speaking. As such, it is important to be prepared. One possible way to prepare is write a full script of your presentation so you know exactly what you want to say. While you do need to know what you are going to say, having a fixed script to follow could actually cause more harm than good. It may be comforting to have a script but it is very difficult to learn a script well enough to be able to deliver it naturally and there is nothing worse than a 'read' presentation. Also, a script may offer a sense of security when the presentation is going well but if something unexpected happens you could lose your place in your script and get stuck trying to remember what comes next.

(Greggs, 2008)

Text 3

When giving a presentation a presenter may have to keep track of a lot of facts and figures, particularly if presenting research data. Rather than having a stack of notes it can be more useful to put the important data that will be discussed in the presentation on the visual aid, e.g. the PowerPoint slide. This is both beneficial for the audience who will be able to see for themselves what the presenter is talking about, and for the presenter, who will be able to look at the visual aid themselves if they need a reminder of a particular piece of data. In fact, the whole of the PowerPoint visuals could be considered as the presenter's notes – there to support the presenter and help the audience.

(Gold, 2008)

Text 4

A good presentation is based on two things. Planning and preparation. In the planning stage you consider the audience and the purpose of your presentation. This helps you focus on what you need to say to those particular people to achieve your purpose. However, the key area in getting ready for a presentation is the preparation. In the planning stage you decide what you want to say, in the preparation stage you become comfortable with how you are going to say it. Good presenters will run through their entire presentation a number of times, trying to make the same point in slightly different ways. This gives them a flexibility of expression so in the live presentation they know they have several ways to say what they want to say.

(Williamson, 2010)

Review of SP 7A – Avoiding Plagiarism

This is a presentation delivered to a group of students which considers the problem of plagiarism and makes suggestions on how plagiarism could be avoided in student work.

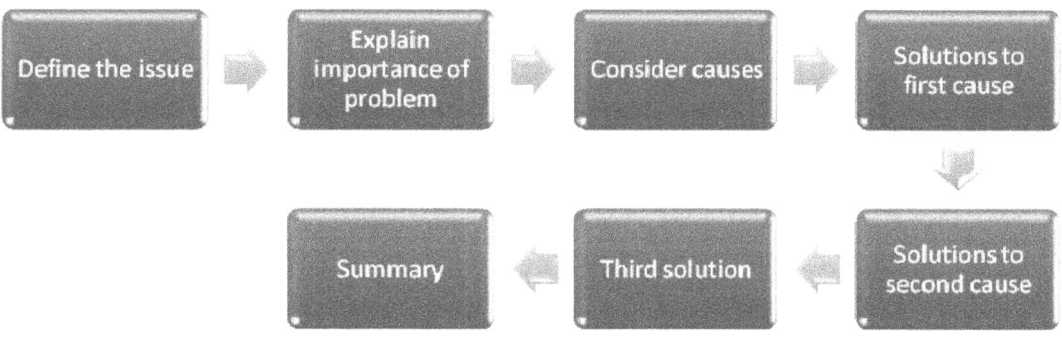

Defining terms

To begin with, I'd like to give you a quick definition of what plagiarism involves and essentially, it's when …

On the most basic level it's …

… a reliance on the source texts. The source texts are …

Explaining importance

So why is … important?

I think the first reason … is important is …

Furthermore, we should …

As I mentioned earlier, it could …

It can be that serious as an issue …

Moving between sections

So moving into …

In terms of the second cause …

And the final thing that I'd say …

So to sum up the presentation …

Discussing solutions

So if we think about the first issue…

(Universities) have an obligation to …

We need to make sure …

For this to be effective I think we need …

There needs to be …

There should be …

And so in terms of the … issue if (summary of solutions) the … issue could be overcome.

Therefore I'd say the solution to this …

(Solution) is therefore a way of overcoming (problem).

The easiest way to avoid (problem) is to …

Dealing with Questions 4

Aside from the obvious problem of having no support in the presentation, the presenter deals with the questions quite well, particularly the third question which suggests a solution the presenter hadn't considered in their presentation.

Question 1 – lack of support/citing in the presentation
The presenter is obviously uncomfortable with the question – laughing and repeating the question sends the wrong message to the audience. However, accepting and acknowledging the weakness in the presentation is the only possible response. If there is something missing in your presentation or if there is a mistake in your logic you realise later, admit it.

Question 2 – plagiarism through laziness
Refocusing the question (asking if it was about motivation) enables the presenter to give a response to this question that builds on one of the main arguments of the presentation and makes a link between raising awareness and motivation.

Question 3 – starting in schools
This is an interesting question – turning towards another possible solution – addressing the question of plagiarism in schools.

Conceding a point
I think in an ideal world then yes, it would begin earlier …

Making a case
… but given that this problem is still happening at university, regardless of what happens in schools, universities still have an obligation to address it.

Comment

This is a difficult presentation to evaluate. In terms of organisation and content, delivery and ideas it is sound. However, the fundamental flaw which would make it an unsuccessful academic presentation is that it is not based on any obvious sources. Without support the presentation becomes an expression of personal opinion and therefore of limited value.

Unit 8
Research Presentations

Unit 8 Research Presentations

Unit Aims

In Unit 3 we looked at some papers about research and in Unit 5 we thought about different research methodologies. In this unit you are going to look at research-based presentations.

- What is the point of a research presentation?
- What should you do in the introduction to a research presentation?
- How can you talk about graphs and tables?

At the end of the unit, return to these questions and see how much your answers may have changed or developed.

In Unit 3 we thought about how research was really a way of building knowledge, to find out something that wasn't known before.

In research, people talk about **finding the gap** and this is really a case of finding out where there is a hole in existing knowledge and then figuring out a way to find the information to fill that hole.

In a research presentation you are trying to show what the gap is and how your research fills it.

Sample Presentation 8A

Watch the Sample Presentation and decide how successfully the presenter explains their research project to the audience.

As an audience member, is there anything else you think should have been included in the presentation to make it easier for you to follow? Make notes below.

Notes

Language Focus

When you are presenting research, you will have to talk about your results. Depending on the type of research you do this might mean talking about statistics and describing tables and graphs.

Learning Presentation 8.1

→ *Statistics, Tables and Graphs*

Watch the Learning Presentation which gives advice about presenting data. As you watch, complete the notes about useful language below.

Discussing Statistics - Statistics can be very powerful in a presentation.

Statistics and fractions give you different ways of expressing the same thing.

- 20% = a fifth = a small minority
- 33% = a third = a sizeable minority
- 50% = half

- 55% = a slight majority
- 75% = three-quarters = the majority
- 90% = the vast majority

However, when using statistics you need to be careful you don't misrepresent data. If you interview two people out of a population of 50 and if they agree on a point, you can't conclude that 100% of the population agree.

Describing Change – You might also need to describe how things changed over time.

went up	went down	shot up	dropped
rebounded	levelled off	fluctuated	topped out

You can also use adverbs to help people see what kind of change you are talking about.

Small or slow change	Large or quick change
moderately slightly gradually steadily slowly	considerably significantly dramatically sharply rapidly quickly suddenly

Remember, when you are presenting data you have to be selective. What are the most important findings you want to highlight?

Presentation Task 10

Now work with a partner and practice presenting the following data.

*Data 1 – You are presenting the sales of Ion Vehicles from 1995-2008. Think of **why** you might want to present this data – what kind of presentation would it fit into?*

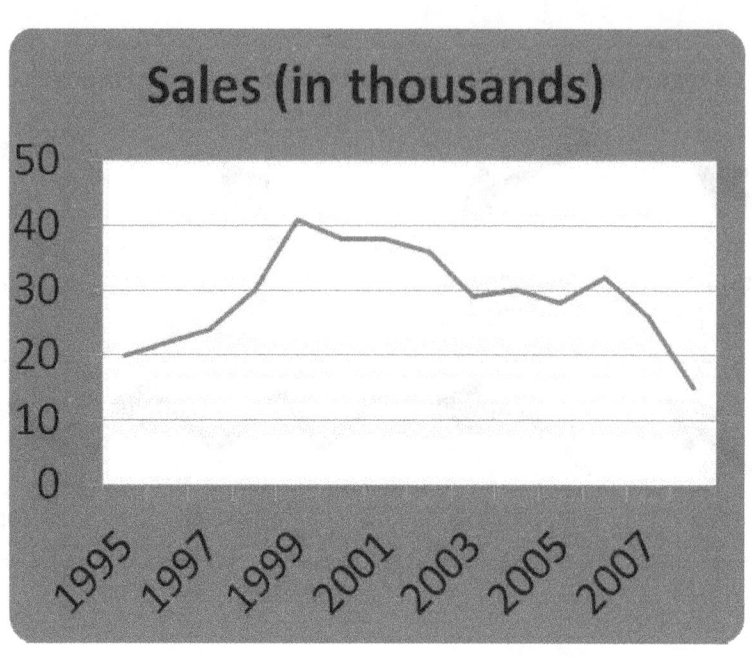

Source: Sales of Ion Vehicles from www.ionmotors.com/sales_history

Data 2 – *You are presenting data about what students do immediately after graduation from a particular university. What kind of presentation could this data support?*

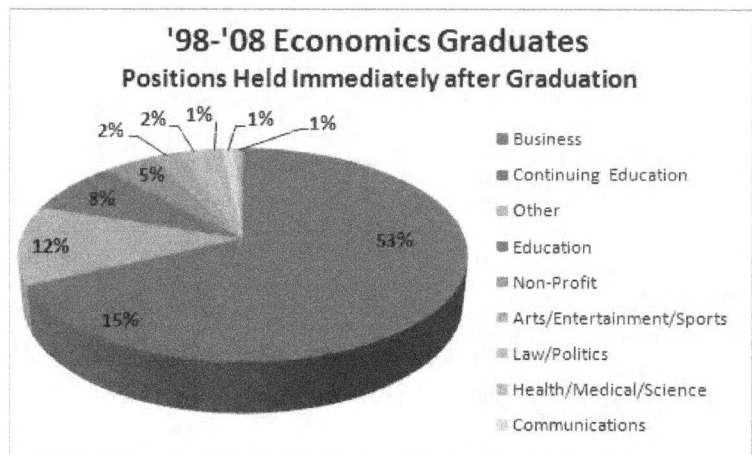

Source: www3.davidson.edu

Learning Presentation 8.2

→ *Finding and Filling A Gap*

A research presentation is about more than just your data. Think about the sample research presentation you watched and think about the structure of it – what the presenter did at each stage of the presentation.

When you have noted as much as you can remember about the organisation of a research presentation, watch the Learning Presentation and add to your notes where necessary.

When you are presenting your smartphone project, you might not have done any primary research. All the information may come from the different sources you have read. However, if you did do any primary research, such as a class survey, for example, make sure you can explain what you did and what you found out, and that you explain it clearly. You might also find yourself having to present research data you have read about. If this is the case, it is still important that the audience understand where the data came from and how it was gathered.

Project Presentation – Giving A Final Presentation

Presentation Task 11
You should now be prepared to give your final Project Presentation. Complete the presentation preparation form below to help you make sure your presentation will be effective.

Audience	
Purpose	
Organisation	
Impact	
Notable	
Theatre	
Support	

Review of SP 8A – Undergraduate Research Methods

This is a presentation of the findings of a research project the presenter did. Its purpose is to show how the situation in one context (US universities) is mirrored in the presenter's own university. The presentation closes with some discussion of the implications of the findings.

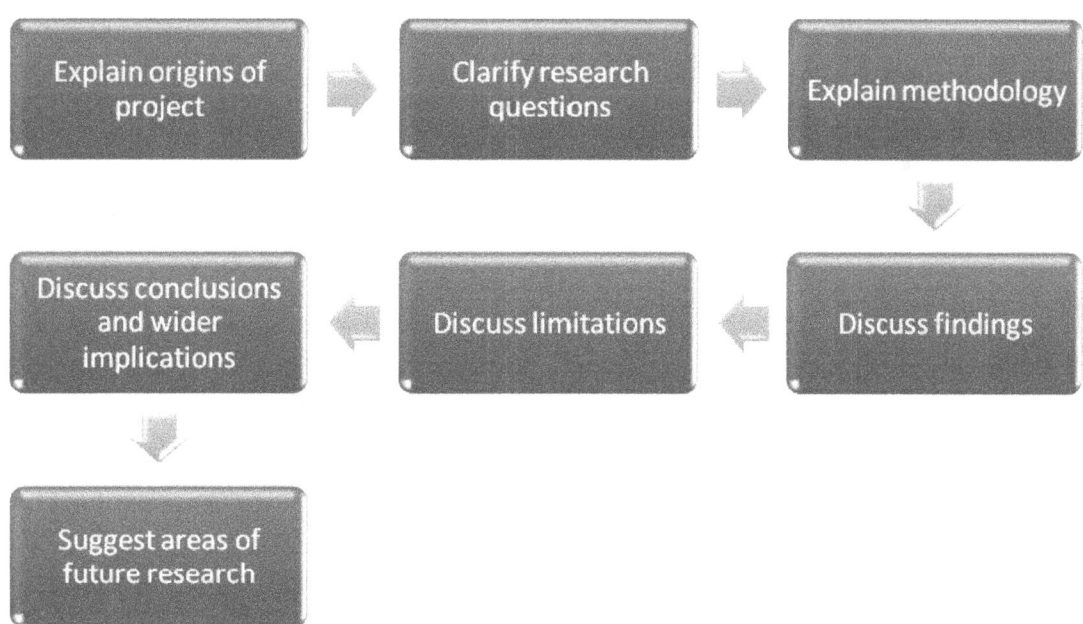

Explaining a research topic

I was looking at …

By this I was looking at …

The thing that got me interested in this was …

I wanted to see whether …

So my research question is based on …

Explaining methodology

The methodology I adopted for this was …

And the (questionnaire) was informed by …

This would give me (statistical) data …

Explaining findings

In terms of ...

There is also ...

What I found interesting about this was ...

As you can see, the majority of them ...

As we can see ...

I had a response rate of ...

Discussing limitations

First of all, it is a small scale study.

There might be ...

It also doesn't show ...

It's also important to know ...

The (motivation behind this) would be interesting to think about.

Discussing conclusions and implications

Having said that, despite those limitations, I think we can come to some conclusions.

In terms of my first research question ...

As to the second question ...

Based on these conclusions ...

I'd also suggest ...

I'd also think ...

Introducing future research topics

I realised what would be very useful would be ...

Similarly, I think we could have ...

Dealing with Questions 5

The presenter seems well prepared and thoroughly familiar with their material, meaning they are able to deal with the questions confidently.

Question 1 – future of libraries
The presenter has a clear opinion on this but the answer is a little circular. The hesitation suggests the presenter is trying to decide how to say what they want to say. Taking a moment to organise the answer would have helped.

Question 2 – e-books
The presenter is in danger of arguing with the questioner here – a difference of opinion is fine but the start of the answer is a little too short and direct. Some form of introduction to the answer like 'I see what you mean' or 'That's an interesting point' would have been better than a direct 'Yes, but'. However, the rest of the answer gives a clear response.

Question 3 – question of methodology – why one discipline?
This is a well answered question. The first part of the answer addresses the advantages of having a smaller test population to make data collection and analysis more effective. The second part of the answer positively suggests that future research is possible and recognises the value of testing the questionnaire before wider use.

Question 4 – clarifying results
One of the issues of discussing data and using statistics is making sure the audience is clear on what those statistics mean. This question could have been avoided by being clearer in the presentation about population size.

Question 5 – follow-up interviews
The presenter deals with this question well, explaining why interviews were not done but appreciating their value and how they could fit in to future research.

Question 6 – reading lists
The presenter acknowledges this was missing from their research (*That wasn't anything I looked into but ...*) but makes the connection with one of their suggested areas of future research.

Comment

The presenter seems comfortable and well informed. He has a clear idea about his project, what the aim was and what he found out. The conclusions and implications seem valid based on the evidence and the suggestions for future research are also directly relevant to the research he conducted.

"Having said that, despite those limitations, I think we can come to some conclusions."

Worksheets

How to use the worksheets

The worksheets that follow can be used with any presentation given during this course or with any academic presentation given outside the context of the course. Some of the worksheets are designed to be used during the preparation stage; others are intended for use by the audience as a means of giving peer-group feedback on a presentation. There is some overlap in the coverage of the sheets so that participants can consider various aspects from slightly different perspectives.

They can also serve as inspiration for independently developed feedback and evaluation forms.

There is no set schedule for the use of these sheets as different students may benefit from different types of feedback at various phases of presenting and practising or might want to focus on different aspects of presenting at different times.

It is important to remember though that a successful presentation is a presentation where all the different aspects of presenting reinforce each other.

Preparation

Title: ....

Presenter(s): ....

Audience	
Purpose	
Organisation	
Impact	
Notable	
Theatre	

Support:

....

....

....

General Feedback

Presenter(s): ....

Topic: ....

Was there a clear introduction?	yes / no
Were the stages of the presentation outlined?	yes / no
Were the different stages signposted?	yes / no
Was there a clear conclusion?	yes / no
Did the speaker ask to take questions?	yes / no
Academic Content	
Was the purpose of the presentation clear?	yes / no
Could you follow the argument presented?	yes / no
Were the main points clearly outlined?	yes / no
Were relevant examples used to support the main idea?	yes / no
Delivery	
Did the presenter use notes effectively?	yes / no
Did the presenter read instead of speaking?	yes / no
Did the presenter make sufficient eye contact?	yes / no
Did the presenter speak clearly?	yes / no
Did the presenter speak loudly enough?	yes / no
Did the presenter speak too fast?	yes / no
Was the accent or pronunciation easy to understand?	yes / no
Comments	
Any other comments or recommendations:	

Overall Assessment

Watch the presentation and complete the table below.

Presenter(s): ....

Use of signposting language				
Suitable for audience				
Clear explanation of terms				
Clear structure				
Use of examples, explanation or evidence to support the main ideas				
Main ideas logically ordered				
Sources mentioned and appropriate				
Clarity of Speech				
Use of speed, volume, stress and pausing				
Makes eye contact / avoids reading text				
Within time limit, appropriate pace and use of pauses				
Visual aids legible / appropriate design				

FURTHER COMMENTS:

Non-verbal Communication

Presenter(s): ……………………………………………………………………………

Does the presenter make regular eye contact?			
Does the presenter make regular eye contact with everyone in the group?			
Where are the speaker's hands usually?			
Are the hand gestures helpful?			
Are there any negative hand gestures? If so, which?			
Does the presenter smile?			
How does the presenter appear to be feeling?	tired? nervous? confident? enthusiastic? Other: …………………		
Does the presenter move around comfortably?			
Are there any distracting movements? If so, which?			
Does the speaker's intonation make the content more interesting?			
Are important content words stressed?			
Further comments:			

Visual Aids

Presenter: ……………………………………………………………………………

Type of Visual Aid: ………………………………………………………………..

Language	
Is the text in note form?	yes / no
Are all of the words spelled correctly?	yes / no
Are capital letters used only when necessary?	yes / no
Is the text punctuated correctly?	yes / no
Will the audience understand the expressions used?	yes / no
Design	
Are the visual aids clear?	yes / no
Does the design suit the presentation?	yes / no
Do any images used benefit the audience?	yes / no
Is the colour scheme attractive?	yes / no
Formatting	
Is the font style consistent?	yes / no
Is the spacing correct and balanced?	yes / no
Is there enough empty space on the slide?	yes / no
Academic Soundness	
Are sources given?	yes / no
Are references provided?	yes / no
Comments	
Any other comments or recommendations:	

Body Language and Delivery

Presenter: ....

Topic: ....

Body Language	
Does the presenter make sufficient eye contact?	yes / no
Does the presenter use hand gestures effectively?	yes / no
Are there any negative hand gestures - what?	yes / no
Does the presenter smile?	yes / no
Does the presenter seem comfortable and confident?	yes / no
Delivery	
Does the presenter use notes effectively?	yes / no
Does the presenter read instead of speaking?	yes / no
Does the presenter speak clearly?	yes / no
Does the presenter speak too fast?	yes / no
Does the speaker's intonation make the content interesting?	yes / no
Are important content words stressed?	yes / no
Comments	
Any other comments or recommendations:	

Dealing with Questions

Presenter: ………………………………………………………………………

Topic: ……………………………………………………………………………..

Reaction to Questions	
Does the presenter seem open to questions?	yes / no
Does the presenter show any nerves in response to questions?	yes / no
Does the presenter encourage questions?	yes / no
Does the presenter seem comfortable and confident?	yes / no
Answers to Questions	
Does the presenter answer the questions effectively?	yes / no
Does the presenter answer the questions directly?	yes / no
Does the questioner seem satisfied with the presenter's answer?	yes / no
Does the presenter have enough topic knowledge to deal with questions?	yes / no
Are the answers an appropriate length?	yes / no
Are the audience engaged during the question section of the presentation?	yes / no
Does the presenter use any negative strategies for dealing with questions?	yes / no
Comments	
Any other comments or recommendations:	

Academic Integrity

Presenter: ……………………………………………………………………………

Topic: ………………………………………………………………………………….

Logic	
Is the purpose of the presentation clear?	yes / no
Does the structure help the presentation achieve its purpose?	yes / no
Is there a clear argument running through the presentation?	yes / no
Does the presenter's conclusion match the argument?	yes / no
Use of Support	
Are important points supported by citations?	yes / no
Are the sources the presenter uses appropriate?	yes / no
Are the sources the presenter uses relevant?	yes / no
Is it clear where data or facts come from?	yes / no
Is it clear how data and facts were gathered?	yes / no
Is the presenter's own position clear?	yes / no
Comments	
Any other comments or recommendations:	

Planning

Presenter: ……………………………………………………………………

Task: ……………………………………………………………………..

Consider the task	
Has your tutor given you a specific task?	
Do you understand the instructions?	
How much time have you got?	
What equipment can you use?	
Who are the audience?	
Are they familiar with your topic?	
How formal do you need to be?	
Ideas	
What do you know already?	
What do you need to learn?	
What is your main focus?	
How many main points have you got?	
Are all your main points *strictly* relevant?	
Are you giving too much detail?	
Planning	
What is the title for your talk?	
Is the overall structure logical?	
Have you got an interesting idea for the introduction?	
Have you thought of a strong conclusion?	
Have you included support (examples, evidence etc.) for the main points?	
Audience	
Have you considered your talk from the audience's point of view?	
Do you need to define any specialist terms?	
Will they find it interesting?	
What do you want the audience to understand and remember?	

Audience Profile

Who are the audience? (age/occupation/gender)	
How many will attend?	
Why will they attend?	
What do they know about the subject? (experts / some knowledge / no knowledge)	
Why might they be interested in the subject?	
What is their relationship to you?	
Are they likely to be tired or sleepy? (early morning/after lunch/end of day)	
What questions do you expect people might ask?	

Notecard Template

Main Idea	No.	Main Idea	No.
Main Idea	No.	Main Idea	No.
Main Idea	No.	Main Idea	No.
Main Idea	No.	Main Idea	No.
Main Idea	No.	Main Idea	No.

Further ELT titles from LinguaBooks

The European Journal of Applied Linguistics and TEFL ISSN: 2192-1032
Edited by Andrzej Cirocki

The *European Journal of Applied Linguistics and TEFL* (EJALTEFL) is a refereed academic publication published twice yearly to disseminate information, knowledge and expertise in applied linguistics with a special focus on English language teaching. This provides a valuable source of reference for linguists, teacher trainers, materials developers and others in the field of EFL/ESL. Each issue offers key insights into current topics, broadening the reader's knowledge and promoting professional development.

In a Strange Land
Short Stories for Creative Learning ISBN: 978-1911369189
By Andrzej Cirocki and Alicia Peña Calvo

IN A STRANGE LAND is a collection of four original short stories which provide teachers with motivating and engaging classroom material at the CEFR B2 to C1 level. This gripping young adult fiction encourages readers to use their imagination and interact with the texts. The stories are supported by creative tasks in which students can integrate all their language skills, use computer technology, practise learning strategies and exercise autonomy.

The stories have been recorded in order to enhance the learning experience and provide greater scope for language learning activities.

The accompanying audio recordings are available as downloads or on two audio CDs and are suitable for both classroom use and listening for pleasure.

LinguaBooks Adult Readers

Each volume in the **LinguaBooks** series of **Short Stories for Adult Learners** and contains five original short stories with accompanying explanations, exercises and extension tasks.

The focus throughout is on authenticity and originality. The language of the stories has not been simplified for easy reading; rather, emergent difficulties are explained in the notes with further activities provided for deeper understanding, extension and autonomous learning. The stories themselves present a varied mix of style and content, ranging from the surprising to the contemplative, with a touch of humour and an occasional hint of pathos.

The language used may be considered equivalent to Level C1 of the Common European Framework of Reference for Languages (CEFR). Taken together with the support activities, however, the book adopts a multilevel approach, featuring exercises at various levels of difficulty, providing scope for consolidation, discovery and autonomous learning. All books in this series are suitable for both classroom use and reading for pleasure.

The following collections of Short Stories for Adult Learners are currently available:

A Busker on Bow Street	ISBN: 978-1911369103
Lost Dreams	ISBN: 978-1911369110
The Farmer's Son	ISBN: 978-1911369127
The Seasonal Visitor	ISBN: 978-1911369134

www.ingramcontent.com/pod-product-compliance
Lightning Source LLC
Chambersburg PA
CBHW082235170426
43196CB00041B/2792